No doubt you've been bombarded with "expert" advice from your parents, professors, and countless advisors. It's time you got advice you can really use— from fellow students who've been where you're headed.

All **Students Helping Students™** guides are written and edited by top students and recent grads from colleges and universities across the U.S. You'll find no preachy or condescending advice here—just stuff to help you succeed in tackling your academic, social, and professional challenges.

Check out these other **Students Helping Students™** titles at your local or college bookstore, and online at Amazon.com, BN.com, Borders.com, and other book retailers!

Each one is packed with practical and useful advice from people who really know what they're talking about— **fellow students who've been where you're headed!**

NAVIGATING YOUR
FRESHMAN YEAR

As if getting accepted wasn't hard enough, dealing with the ups and downs of your first year at college is a unique challenge you'll be glad you only have to face once. Pick up this guide and learn from the first-hand experiences of dozens of college students who've survived their freshman year and lived to help you get through it without losing your mind. *($8.95)*

LEAPING FROM PUBLIC HIGH
TO A TOP U.

You worked your butt off for years to do well in school and be accepted by a top university. Congratulations. But if you think that the toughest part is behind you, think again. Get advice from fellow students who've done what you're about to do. Pick up this guide to help you prepare for and tackle the academic, social, and personal challenges that you'll face as you make the transition from high school to a top university. *($6.95)*

TACKLING YOUR FIRST
COLLEGE PAPER

Whether you wrote dozens of papers in high school or escaped without writing more than a few, acing your first few college papers will be a new and challenging experience. This guide will help you get ready, get organized, choose an interesting topic and a strong thesis, write a clear and error-free paper, and keep your sanity while you do it. *($6.95)*

FISHING FOR
A MAJOR

You might know exactly what you want to do with your life. Or you might have no idea at all. In either case, reading what other students think about finding a major that makes you happy can help you consider things you've not thought of. Find out how other students approach choosing classes, getting the best out of the advising system, thinking about a career and finding a passion—and you might discover more than just a college major. *($6.95)*

SCORING A
GREAT INTERNSHIP

Finding and getting a killer internship during college has no downside— you'll learn a ton, spice up your resume, meet new people, and hopefully get a few steps closer to knowing what you'd like to do with your life after college. This guide is packed with tips on how to find the best internships, get yourself noticed and accepted, and learn the most once you're there. *($6.95)*

FINDING YOUR PASSION
BEYOND COLLEGE ACADEMICS

Part of what college is all about is helping us to figure out what we like to do and what we might like to do with our lives. To really do this, you have to go beyond classes and academics, and explore your passions by getting involved in extracurriculars. Think you might like to be a journalist but hate your English class? Become a reporter for your college or local town paper. A life as a psychologist sounds like fun? You won't learn much about it in your psych class, but you might if you staff a counseling hotline. Pick up this guide and use it to help you find your passion. *($6.95)*

TACKLING YOUR
HIGH SCHOOL TERM PAPER

You won't escape high school without writing at least a few term papers. Whether you're a naturally talented writer or would rather go to the dentist than write a paper, pick up this guide to learn the best way to tackle your term papers. Written by students who've written more than a few papers in high school, this guide will help you get organized, choose the best topic, formulate your main arguments, research effectively, and write a clear and error-free paper. *($6.95)*

To learn more about **Students Helping Students™** guides, read samples and student-written articles, share your own experiences with other students, suggest a topic or ask questions, visit us at **www.StudentsHelpingStudents.com**!

We're always looking for fresh minds and new ideas!

Students Helping Students™

GETTING THROUGH COLLEGE WITHOUT GOING BROKE

First Edition

NATAVI GUIDES

New York

Getting Through College Without Going Broke.
First Edition.

Published by **NATAVI GUIDES**. For information on bulk purchases or custom promotional guides, please contact the publisher via email at sales@nataviguides.com or by phone at 1.866.425.4218. You can learn more about our promotional guides program on our website, www.nataviguides.com.

Cover design by Monica Baziuk.

Printed in the U.S.A.

ISBN 1-932204-01-6

Library of Congress Cataloging-in-Publication Data

Fives, Theresa.
   Getting through college without going broke.-- 1st ed.
      p. cm. -- (Students helping students)
Written by Theresa Fives with the collaboration of Holly Popowski.
   ISBN 1-932204-01-6 (pbk.)
   1. College student orientation--United States--Handbooks, manuals, etc. 2. College students--United States--Finance, Personal--Handbooks, manuals, etc. 3. Education, Higher--United States--Finance. I. Popowski, Holly. II. Natavi Guides (Firm) III. Title. IV. Series.
   LB2343.32.F58 2003
   378'.198--dc21

                                        2002156577

A NOTE FROM THE FOUNDERS OF STUDENTS HELPING STUDENTS™:

Dear Reader,

Welcome to Students Helping Students™!

Before you dive head-first into reading this book, we wanted to take a moment to share with you where Students Helping Students™ came from and where we're headed.

It was only a few years ago that we graduated from college, having made enough mistakes to fill a *War and Peace*-sized novel, learned more and different things than we expected going in, and made some tough decisions—often without having enough advice to help us out. As we thought about our college experiences, we realized that some of the best and most practical advice we ever got came from our classmates and recent grads. It didn't take long for the light bulb to go on: We started a publishing company and launched the Students Helping Students™ series.

Our vision for Students Helping Students™ is simple: Allow high school and college students to learn from fellow students who can share brutally honest and practical advice based on their own experiences. We've designed our books to be brief and to the point—we've been there and know that students don't have a minute to waste. They are extremely practical, easy to read, and cheap, so they don't empty your wallet.

As with all firsts, we're bound to do some things wrong, and if you have reactions or ideas to share with us, we can't wait to hear them. Visit **www.StudentsHelpingStudents.com** to submit your comments online and find our contact information.

Thanks for giving us a shot. We hope that the student advice in this book will make your life better and easier.

Nataly and Avi
Founders of NATAVI GUIDES and Students Helping Students™

the primary author

Theresa Fives is a linguistics major at Cornell University, and is a member of the class of 2004. She is well-experienced with the ins and outs of paying for an expensive education. She receives several scholarships and grants and has worked both part- and full-time jobs for several years to afford college. She hopes that you'll find this guide useful and the mistakes she made won't have been in vain.

the collaborator

Holly Popowski started her education as a communications major at the University of Minnesota - Duluth, and then transferred to New York University, majoring in philosophy. She has run the gamut in terms of aid, finding ways to pay her way through school via scholarships, grants, loans, fighting the financial aid office, and taking up jobs. Holly has lived every financial nightmare known to man, but she fully intends to graduate in 2003.

the contributors

Students from Bard College, Columbia University, Cornell University, Dartmouth College, Emory University, George Mason University, Harvard University, Hunter College, Middlebury College, New York University, Northeastern University, Orange County Community College, Princeton University, State University of New York - Albany, State University of New York - Buffalo, Trinity College, University of Minnesota - Duluth, University of Pennsylvania, University of Texas - El Paso, University of Wisconsin - Madison, University of Wisconsin - Oshkosh, Wesleyan University, Winona State University, and Wittenberg University contributed to this guide.

author's note

Before you start reading, I wanted to share with you what I tried to accomplish by putting together this guide.

This book does not just offer you information on how to apply for financial aid and scholarships. That's extremely important, but it's just one part of what goes into being able to pay for an often expensive college education. We've also included advice and tips on things like finding a job that you can balance with academics, creating a realistic budget and sticking to it, learning how to take advantage of credit cards without going into debt, and many other aspects of what you'll have to do to get through college without going broke.

This is not an unrealistic guide to managing your money. We won't tell you to do things that we know you're never going to do, like save every penny you earn or never buy anything unless it's on sale—this may be sage advice, but it's just not realistic. We've been there and so have dozens of contributors of advice to this guide, and we know exactly what you're going through. If we've included advice in this book it's only because we've tried it and know that it works.

Hopefully, our combined effort will help to make the daunting task of financing your college education a bit more manageable and your college experience that much more enjoyable. You CAN do it!

- Theresa

collaborator's note

Simply because you bought this book, don't expect to escape college without ever worrying about money and paying for school again. We can't solve the problem of paying for an expensive college education for you. All we can do is offer suggestions that we learned the hard way and the best way—by going through the experience and making enough mistakes to learn from them.

Within these pages you'll find helpful tips on navigating the world of loans, scholarships, monthly bills, and other things you have to get to know to make it through college on a budget. We've tried to be realistic and practical in our advice because advice you can't actually follow is pretty useless. We've also tried to give you some comfort by bringing to you our and our contributors' personal failures and triumphs. You're not alone as you go through this.

Good luck, and spend wisely!

- Holly

contents

what it is

Financing your college education is overwhelming. It is a challenge. It is about determination and hard work. It is about exhausting every possible option. It will make your hand sore from all the essays you'll write, and at times you'll wonder if the search for yet another scholarship is really worth it. Paying for school requires organization and responsibility and maturity. It will require you to be frugal and often give up things that you want.

But figuring out how to pay for your college education is a great investment in your future. Not only will you get a great education, but you'll learn how to be resourceful, how to manage your money, and how to prioritize where you spend it. Skills like that are even more essential after you graduate. Financing your education is one of those aspects of college life that really will teach you meaningful lessons and skills for your future.

Finding a way to pay for your education and working your butt off to do it is a choice. You don't have to go to an expensive private university. Many great community and state colleges can give you a solid education, if you make the most of your time there. Think about your goals and your and your family's resources, get as much advice as possible, and make the choice that makes the most sense to you.

what it's not

The most important thing to remember is that financing your college education is not impossible. You've probably looked at the costs of attending some of the expensive private schools and wondered how on earth you were going to pay those bills and still have time and money left for a life. It's pretty overwhelming. But it's also something that millions of college students—like us—tackle year after year. As long as you have the determination and drive to be responsible and work hard, you can find a way to do it.

Of course, financing your college education isn't easy. Money is not out there looking for you, and, as we've all heard time and again, money certainly does not grow on trees. You do actually have to get up and go out there yourself and look for it. We won't lie to you—this can be difficult, and it probably won't be fun. Acting like an adult is not as much fun as acting like a teenager.

But no matter how annoying and frustrating it may get, remember that financing your college education is not a waste of time, and you'll probably spend the rest of your life proud of your accomplishments. It would be nice if you had every resource in the world and didn't have to worry about paying thousands of dollars a year to get an education, but it's as nice to know that you can tackle this challenge.

planning for college

Before you start applying to colleges—before you even start to seriously think about which colleges you want to apply to—you have to start thinking about how you'll pay for your education. Very few families have vast resources, and figuring out how to finance your college education will take a lot of organization and hard work. It's not impossible, but you need to start early so that you take advantage of every possible opportunity.

Even if by the time you pick up this book you're already well on your way to applying for financial aid and sending out your college acceptance letters—or have even started school—you can still learn a few important things to help you get through college on a budget and graduate without extra debt. It's truly never too late.

Here are some tips to get you on the right track.

START SAVING EARLY
▼
TALK TO YOUR PARENTS
▼
MAKE FRIENDS IN THE RIGHT PLACES
▼
CONSIDER A VARIETY OF SCHOOLS

START SAVING EARLY

"The summer before your freshman year, try not to spend as much money going out. I used to go out to eat all the time and it was such a waste of money."

**Sophomore,
SUNY - Albany**

If you have a part-time or summer job during high school, it's a good idea to begin putting money away for college as soon as possible. It may be too late by the time you're reading this book to take full advantage of this advice, but even if you just start now, it will help you later. You may end up using this saved money to help pay for tuition or books, you may just keep it for extra spending money, or maybe you'll buy a new computer for yourself, but no matter what you decide to do with it, it will help.

collaborator's corner
▼
Up until now, you've probably been using whatever money you make for personal stuff like going out, buying clothes, CDs, or whatever else you like. I worked very hard throughout high school and made about $5,000 a year. By the time I went off to college, I had nothing saved. I looked back and tried to figure out on what I'd spent so much money: car, gas, dates, times with friends, CDs, and books. By the time I got to college, it all seemed like such a waste. As hard as it can be, you need to decide early what is more important: a new pair of jeans or an extra $75 in the bank that will pay for several meals in college.
▲

Open a savings account near your home and put a certain percentage of every paycheck into the bank. If you put it into the bank, rather than just saving a pile of cash under your mattress, you won't be as tempted to spend it. Plus, you'll earn interest, which can add up.

Here's an important caveat that you need to know about your savings:

Colleges will expect you to contribute a certain percentage of your savings to pay for tuition and room and board, and that percentage usually represents a considerable share of your savings. When colleges calculate how much financial aid you should receive, they determine the appropriate amount—we'll talk in detail about this a bit later—and then subtract a portion of your savings from it. The more savings you have, the less financial aid you'll get.

So if you're planning on using your savings for something like a new computer, buy the computer before you fill out financial aid forms. This way, you won't have to claim as savings money that you'll be spending very soon anyway.

TALK TO YOUR PARENTS

Finances are a touchy subject that you and your parents may be uncomfortable talking about, but it's really important to be open and honest. Ask your parents if they have any money saved for your education. Find out how much they can realistically afford to pay for college each year, and how much they'll expect you to contribute. Understanding your family's financial situation is important, and you shouldn't assume anything at all without talking about it first.

If your family can't contribute much to paying for your college education, it doesn't mean that you should rule out expensive private universities. You will likely qualify for significant financial aid and scholarships based on financial need. But knowing exactly what your and your family's resources are will help you determine what type of aid and how much you'll need to get.

You may have older brothers and sisters who have gone through this process before, making your parents old pros. If not, make sure that everyone is on the same page with who is going to pay for what, what applications need to get filled out, and when and who will do it. The college search and application process can be overwhelming and stressful, and the more you help yourself and your family to communicate and get organized, the easier it will be.

author's corner
▼

I was lucky because my mother really wanted to be involved in the college search. In fact, she was usually a lot more involved than I was. Sometimes, it would get on my nerves, but I'm grateful that she took care of so much. She knew when all the applications and forms were due, she told me what to fill out and when I had to sign something, she made sure everything got done on time. She probably talked to my high school guidance counselor more than I did! If your parents are like this, don't feel like they're interfering and don't be resentful. If your parents seem like the exact opposite of this, you can try to get them more involved, but know when to take control and handle it on your own.
▲

MAKE FRIENDS IN THE RIGHT PLACES

This may seem silly, but it will help you to make friends with certain people in your community who might have some say over where scholarship money goes. Get to know your guidance counselor, your high school principal, and the teachers in your school. Remember: Guidance counselors are there to help you find resources to pay for college. They have a ton of financial aid information and might know of scholarships you can't find on your own. They may also have a say in how certain local scholarships get awarded, so making sure they know who you are, how great you are, and how hard you're working to find money for school isn't a bad idea.

> *"One of the most important contacts I ever made was with my high school counselor. When it came time for scholarships and she was reading through hundreds of applications, my name stuck out because we had shared a lot of discussions about college."*
>
> **Senior,**
> **New York University**

If you have a job in your town or if you do community service work, you'll probably meet local business people. All of these people could potentially influence local scholarship money. Having connections could definitely pay off for you. Literally.

Imagine applying for a scholarship given out by a local business association, and then competing for it against a classmate who has waited tables for two years at a local restaurant. Chances are, some people in the association have dined at this restaurant and have become acquainted with the other student. If he knows what he's doing, this student has probably also made a good impression. Would you rather be him, or would you rather compete against him for a scholarship?

CONSIDER A VARIETY OF SCHOOLS

"Take the time to apply to lots of schools. Everyone knows this is a good idea if you want to maximize your chances of being admitted, but it's also the best insurance policy you can have against financial aid disasters. If your dream school comes back with an offer to put your whole family into indentured servitude for life, you'll have a fallback position, and you'll also have some leverage."

**Recent Grad,
Dartmouth College**

Your decision of where to apply to college will be influenced by many factors—how far away from home the college is, what academic programs it has, what the social scene is like, whether it's in a small town or big city, how many students are enrolled, and a number of other factors that differ greatly from person to person. The cost of attending each school should also make it on this list.

Don't ever rule out your choice of college based on how expensive it is. If you work very hard, are persistent, and know where to look, you can find a way to pay for it.

You've probably heard this piece of advice over and over, but take our word for it—most of us are living testaments to the possibility of attending an expensive school without being related to Bill Gates.

What you should do is make sure that you apply to a range of colleges—very expensive, moderate, and less expensive. Some people do everything right and still can't find enough money to afford their dream school. When this happens, it's important to have a backup school, a financial safety school, which you know you'll be able to afford even if you don't get the right financial aid package.

Here are some stats we think you should know. It's not so you feel intimidated, but so you know the size of the challenge you're trying to tackle.

- According to the College Board, the average cost of attending a private four-year university during the 2001-2002 academic year was $17,000 in tuition and fees, and an additional $6,500 in room and board.

- The cost of attending a four-year public university during the same academic year was $3,800 for tuition, and $5,300 for room and board. Public colleges and universities are significantly cheaper, and you should apply to at least one. Many have great academics and rich extracurricular opportunities, and some are among the top universities in the country—University of Michigan and University of Virginia are two great examples.

If you'd like to go out of state, but don't want to pay a lot more for college, do some research into reciprocity agreements that your state might have with neighboring states. Some will charge you in-state tuition if you go to a state university and live in a neighboring state.

collaborator's corner

▼

One of the most important factors in my decision of which school to go to was that it had to be out of state. But I also realized that colleges have in-state and out-of-state tuition prices, the latter being double the cost of the former. I checked into it, and in Wisconsin, they had reciprocity agreements with five other states, so I could go to any of those state schools for the in-state tuition rate.

▲

☞ COVER YOUR BASES

Here's a simple template we thought could help you organize your college choices while keeping financial aid in mind. Once you figure out your preliminary list of colleges, go through and rank each one in terms of difficulty of getting in and the cost of attendance. Your goal is to make sure that you apply to one or two schools where you're pretty likely to get in and that you can afford.

Name of College	Difficulty of Getting In	Cost of Attendance*
	Reach, Likely, Safety	High, Moderate, Low
College A		
College B		
College C		
College D		
College E		
College F		

*Later we talk about all of the calculations that should go into figuring out how much it will actually cost you to attend a particular school.

WE TALK WITH...

Hope Roth
Junior, Trinity College

How many schools did you apply to, and how did their financial aid offers affect your decision on which school to go to?

I applied to eleven schools and got into five (Trinity, Oberlin, Lafayette, Evergreen State College, and UMass Amherst). Financial aid was a major factor in my decision. One school didn't even give me enough to cover room and board, let alone tuition. Other schools gave me nice aid packages, but none of them was as generous as Trinity. Not only did they give me all the money recommended by the standard guidelines, but they also converted my loans and work-study into grants.

If you had your education to do all over again, what would you change financially?

I would have saved more of my paychecks from my campus job. I would have dropped the campus meal plan sooner. I'm cooking for myself this semester and I'm saving a lot of money and eating better. I also would have stopped ordering out sooner. Late night pizza and Chinese food thinned out my wallet and had the reverse effect on my waistline.

Over the years, how did you notice your aid package change?

My award has gone up slightly since I matriculated because there was a slight tuition increase at Trinity and because my family's financial situation got slightly worse.

Do you have any advice for students trying to pick a school?

Visit schools as early on in the process as you can. I was sure that I would get into my top choice, so I never visited any of my middle range or safety schools. Then, when I only got into my middle range and safeties, I had three weeks to decide where to go and no visits under my belt. That made for a stressful April.

☞ EARLY DECISION

If you're thinking of applying Early Decision to a particular college or university, make sure that you understand the implications it has for financial aid. While you'll know if you're accepted by early winter, you won't receive your financial aid award until the spring, most likely in March or April, when admission letters for regular admission are sent out. <u>This means that you'll have to accept your offer of admission to your Early Decision school before you know what your financial aid award will be.</u>

This is very important. If you do get into your Early Decision school and accept the offer of admission, you're stuck with whatever financial aid package the school provides to you. Most colleges and universities use what's called Need-Blind Admission—meaning that they don't take your financial need into account when deciding whether to give you an offer. In many cases, schools will give you enough financial aid to make up the difference between your family's expected contribution (more on this later) and the cost of attending that particular school, but there are many exceptions. And as we mention in the following sections, what the government and the school might estimate as your family's ability to pay may not always agree with your own assessment.

Don't rule out Early Decision just on this basis, but do think about it seriously. What you should definitely do is make sure that you're pretty certain that your Early Decision school is your number one choice. You may also want to consider applying Early Option (or Action), which some schools offer and which does not require that you enroll if you're accepted.

finding money

All right, so now you've been looking at colleges and you probably know where you want to apply. You might be nervous if you're applying to some expensive schools, but don't worry—there is financial aid out there for you and we're going to help you get it.

The one thing that we can tell you for certain about financial aid is that you have to work hard to get it. It would be nice if it all worked out on its own and someone came to your door with a full four-year scholarship, but that doesn't happen. You have to fill out forms, keep track of deadlines, write essays, check into dozens of resources, and do this not just before you go to college, but also while you're there. It's a hassle and it's tiring, but persistence does pay off.

GET ORGANIZED
▼
START EARLY
▼
TALK TO YOUR GUIDANCE COUNSELOR
▼
NAIL THE FAFSA
▼
ACE YOUR SCHOLARSHIP APPLICATONS
▼
NAVIGATE THE LOAN MAZE
▼
LOOK UNDER EVERY ROCK
▼
DON'T MISS DEADLINES
▼
DON'T RELY ON YOUR PARENTS
▼
SAY THANK YOU

GET ORGANIZED

Looking for money to pay for college is a time-consuming and often frustrating process, and getting organized before you start can help keep you sane as you go through it. It will also ensure that you don't miss an important step or a deadline that ends up costing you money.

To help you get organized here's a general overview of the three main types of things you'll have to do as you go through the not-always-fun process of looking for money:

- Fill out required financial aid forms: FAFSA and PROFILE are the most common, and you'll have to fill them out if you plan to apply for any type of financial aid, including loans and need-based scholarships. You'll need your and your parents' most recent tax returns to fill out the required financial information.

- Search for scholarships: This is one of the most time consuming but also potentially the most rewarding parts of finding money to pay for college. You should plan on searching and applying for local, national, and special interest scholarships.

- Learn about your loan options: There are many different kinds of loans for which you could be eligible and you should spend some time researching and understanding each option.

On the next page is a timeline of when you should try to complete each of the main steps.

☞ FINANCIAL AID MILESTONES

Here's a list of the key steps you'll have to take in applying for financial aid. We'll talk about each one in detail in this chapter, but you can use this checklist to help you get organized. The timing we suggest here is approximate, and you should check with each of the schools where you're applying to ensure that it doesn't have different deadlines.

JUNIOR YEAR

✓ Research colleges to ensure that you'll be applying to a variety of schools both in terms of academic rigor and cost.

✓ Begin to research scholarships to understand what your options are. The summer before your senior year is a great time to put in some grunt work.

SENIOR YEAR

Fall

✓ Apply to a variety of schools and make sure not to rule out any simply because they're expensive.

✓ Talk to your guidance counselor and your parents about your financial aid requirements and your strategy for completing the required forms and applying for scholarships.

✓ Begin to apply for scholarships and grants. The earlier you apply, the more time you'll have to apply to as many as possible.

January

✓ File the FAFSA. Some schools require that you submit it by the end of February, so pay attention to deadlines.

✓ File the PROFILE or other custom forms required by the colleges to which you're applying.

✓ Continue to apply for scholarships.

February

✓ If you filed the FAFSA in early January, you'll receive your Student Aid Report (SAR).

✓ Check your SAR for errors and send in any required corrections.

April

✓ The majority of your acceptance letters and financial aid award letters arrive, which outline what financial aid package each school offers.

✓ Carefully compare each of the financial aid packages you receive, paying attention to total amount of aid, the left-over amount your family will have to pay, and what the aid is made up of—loans, scholarships, grants, work-study, etc.

✓ Contact schools to ask for more aid. Unless you've received a full scholarship, you and your parents should ask for more money.

May

✓ Choose your school and make sure to send in all of the required financial aid paperwork.

✓ Fill out any required applications for student and parent loans, as well as private loans, if you didn't receive enough financial aid from your school.

START EARLY

The sooner you start looking for money for college and filling out applications and forms, the better off you'll be. No question. If you and your parents file taxes early in the year, instead of waiting until April, you'll have the most up-to-date information about the state of your family's finances for the FAFSA and PROFILE forms. Writing scholarship essays early will let you be more relaxed, and will give you time to have your mom, your little brother, your English teacher, and anyone else who's willing read them over and make them better. Some scholarships also have early deadlines, and you don't want to miss out on extra cash just because you didn't find out about it in time.

You should start learning about all of the available financial aid options during your junior year, and be ready to write your scholarship essays and submit applications by the first semester of your senior year. It's not a bad idea to write a few scholarship essays during the summer after your junior year, and if you're working on your college essays at the same time, you can probably re-use some of the material. You'll fill out your FAFSA and PROFILE forms at the beginning of your second semester senior year, and you'll get your financial aid offers around the same time as your college acceptance letters in the spring.

As long as you're starting early, check in with students who graduated the year before you. Find out who won the biggest scholarships and ask them for advice and perhaps even to look over your essay. Not everyone will want to help, but it can't hurt to ask and any advice you can get is useful.

TALK TO YOUR GUIDANCE COUNSELOR

It is your guidance counselor's job to help you plan for college and advise you on how to pay for it. Guidance counselors have lists of local and national scholarships, as well as resources for searching for scholarships. From experience of working with many other students they also know which colleges are more likely to give you a decent financial aid package, and they can recommend to you where to look for other financing options.

Set up a meeting with your guidance counselor during your junior year to talk about your plan of attack to find money for college, and continue to meet with him or her throughout the process. The more you talk to your counselor, the more he or she will remember your name, and the more he or she will realize your determination to find a way to pay for college. Your counselor will remember this when he or she is meeting with local scholarship committees, and it can help you in the long run.

"I talked often with my guidance counselor about my family's fear of not being able to pay for college. It must have stuck in her mind because she kept telling me about all these scholarships, and even recommended me for some of them."

Recent Grad,
Wesleyan University

If you find that your counselor isn't being very helpful—it happens—then you have to find other people who can give you advice. You probably won't be able to switch to a different counselor, but you should talk to your teachers, your principal, and other guidance counselors and ask for their help. You need good advice and you have to work hard to get it.

NAIL THE FAFSA

"My parents did most of the filling in of financial aid forms, but I wish I had done more. Now that I'm paying hundreds of dollars a month to pay back the loans, I feel like the band that never read the fine print and was signed to a bad record deal."

Recent Grad,
University of Wisconsin - Madison

Even if you don't think that you'll be eligible for financial aid, you should apply. It can't hurt to try, and you won't have a shot at any aid if you don't file the required applications. You don't have to be poor to receive financial aid, and many families lose out on thousands of dollars in loans and scholarships because they think they have too much money to qualify. Don't miss out on aid that can save you thousands.

The first and most important thing you need to do is fill out the **Free Application for Federal Student Aid**—or, as it's widely known, the FAFSA.

- This is the bedrock of all financial aid forms—without it you can't get any aid at all—so it's extremely important that you file it on-time and accurately. There is no filing fee, and you can file this form online if you wish. We suggest that you take the opportunity to file the FAFSA electronically by going to **www.fafsa.ed.gov**. You'll get your Student Aid Report sooner and since the online form has internal checks built in, you'll avoid careless errors. If you do want to fill out the paper version, you can usually get it from your school or by calling 1-800-4-FED-AID.

- You need to re-file the FAFSA every year that you are in school in order to be considered for federal student aid, including grants, loans and work-study programs. Often schools use this form to determine non-federal aid as well. A change in your family's financial situation may increase or decrease the amount of aid you're receiving, and even if you didn't qualify one year you might be eligible for aid the following year.

- You should file the FAFSA early during the second semester of your senior year. You can't file it before January 1—you need to give the government the full picture of your family's financial situation for the most recent fiscal year—but you should file it soon after that. The Department of Education will process FAFSA forms all year while you're in college, but most school aid is distributed on a first come first serve basis, so it's in your interest to apply early. In addition, each school has a different priority deadline, many as early as February or March, and you need to meet that deadline to get your full potential aid. It's not necessary to submit your and your parents' tax return to the IRS before submitting your FAFSA, but since you will need some important information from your and your parents' taxes while filling it out, you should try to complete them beforehand.

- The FAFSA asks for details of your finances from both you and your parents, but you don't have to turn in your actual tax forms to your school or with the FAFSA. To ensure honesty, however, colleges do random audits where they check your information, and you risk losing all your aid if the information you supply to FAFSA does not match your filed tax forms.

It takes about six weeks for your FAFSA to be processed, and you'll then be sent a **Student Aid Report (SAR)**. This report can look a bit confusing, but it's not so bad. The front page will have the date and something called the **Expected Family Contribution** (EFC), which will be followed by a number. That number is the amount of dollars that your family will be expected to contribute to your college education each year. The lower the amount, the more aid you'll likely receive. Here's an easy way to think about it:

Financial Need=Cost of Attendance–Expected Contribution

However, having a low expected contribution does not guarantee full aid. If your EFC is only $500, but you're applying to schools that cost $20,000, don't necessarily expect your financial aid package to fully cover the difference.

"My parents gasped when they looked at the expected contribution—it seemed ridiculously high. It was kind of panicky for a while, but we talked to the school where I really wanted to go, explained our circumstances, and they were able to give me some loans. Not ideal, but it was a solution."

**Recent Grad,
Wesleyan University**

Make sure you read your SAR carefully and review it for any errors you may have made. If you note any errors, make corrections on Part 2 of the form and mail it back promptly—you'll receive a new SAR. The federal processor of the FAFSA will send a copy of your SAR to each of the schools that you listed on the FAFSA and they will use it to calculate your financial aid package.

Some schools require further paperwork than the FAFSA. They'll ask that you fill out their custom form or something called the PROFILE. The PROFILE is also administered by the College Board and is used by many private colleges to determine your eligibility for non-governmental loans such as those provided by the school itself. The PROFILE is more in-depth than the FAFSA and uses a different methodology to calculate your financial need. To file the PROFILE online, go to **profileonline.collegeboard.com**. Make sure to check with each of the schools to which you're applying to see if you need to file a PROFILE, or if there are any other forms you should worry about.

Many high schools offer information sessions for seniors on applying for aid and filling out the proper forms. If yours does, take advantage of them, and bring your parents. It's not the most fun you'll ever have, but the more help you get in this process, the better off you are.

collaborator's corner

▼

Not every student can turn to their parents to fill out forms or help them out financially. In this situation, talk to your school about becoming an "independent student." The process for doing so is different at every college, but if it's something you can do, then you won't need to report your parents' income on your FAFSA, and their income won't be counted in what the government expects you to pay. This is often a last resort option at schools and many will only allow you to use it in extreme circumstances.

▲

WE TALK WITH...

Austin Brown
Junior, Hunter College

Did you feel that transferring schools helped or hurt your financial aid, or made no difference at all?

I wasn't eligible for financial aid at the private university where I went for two years, and while I'm still not eligible for aid, the amount that I'm now paying at City College is manageable enough, and I realized that it's not worth applying for loans and ending up paying four times what I borrowed.

Part way through your education you got married, which changed your dependent status. Did this do anything to help your financial aid package with your school?

Somehow, I seem to have missed the financial aid boat every time. Actually, I did re-file FAFSA after I got married, but it didn't make any difference. Even though I filled it out very carefully and accurately, they sent me a letter saying that there were inconsistencies in my application—I'm not sure what that meant. Honestly, I suppose that someone more diligent would have fought for it since technically once you're married you're not considered a dependent of your parents.

If you could start college all over again, what would you do differently that would have affected your financial situation?

Generally, I don't like to think about what I might have been— you've got to work with the choices you've already made. But I suppose I would have liked to know more about CUNY and what a great university it is, and I might have wanted to go there from the start. Then again, had I done that, I wouldn't have met my wife and I wouldn't have had to make the difficult but fulfilling decision of starting out again, financially independent from my parents.

ACE YOUR SCHOLARSHIP APPLICATIONS

You should apply for as many scholarships as humanly possible if you're serious about getting through college without a load of debt. Chances are you will have to take out some loans, but the more scholarships you have the less debt will weigh you down after you graduate. Scholarships are the best kind of financial aid you can get because you don't need to pay them back.

Over one billion dollars is given out in the form of scholarships each year to undergraduate students. That's a lot of money. You can earn a scholarship for all sorts of things—if you do well in school, write a certain essay, play a certain sport, speak a certain language, come from a certain racial or ethnic background, have a family member in the armed forces, plan to go into a certain field after college, or possess any number of other qualifications. Each year, many national foundations and corporations give away thousands of dollars in scholarship money that could be yours.

"I applied for LOTS of scholarships. The problem was, I applied for the general ones, the ones that are for "high school seniors and juniors" and "women under 35 with leadership potential." Everyone has something unique about him or her, be it an interest in community service, religion, sports, ethnicity, or another characteristic. Look it up—there is probably a scholarship for it!"

**Freshman,
Emory University**

We won't even attempt to list scholarships here because there are great resources where you can easily search for them. Our favorite—and the biggest and most popular—is FastWeb (**www.fastweb.com**). You can search based on your background and profile and find scholarships best suited for you. For a more detailed list of some good places to search for scholarships, check the **"helpful resources"** section at the end of this guide.

The local businesses and organizations in your town will also give out many types of scholarships. Talk to your guidance counselor or financial aid officer about where you can find applications for these scholarships and go after them.

Go after any scholarship that you even remotely qualify for, regardless of how small the amount. Every little bit helps, and often, there's less competition for smaller scholarships. And remember to continue to apply for scholarships even after you begin attending college. Often we're motivated during the application process and don't keep at it later on. It's worth your time.

author's corner
▼

All throughout my senior year of high school, I applied for countless scholarships. I wrote essays about why I wanted to go to college, who my biggest role model was, what my Italian-American heritage has meant to me, and even why I thought Burger King symbolized the American Dream. I wrote my name, address, and social security number so many times, I thought I'd scream. In the end, I didn't even get close to half the number of scholarships I'd applied for. But, because I'd applied for so many, I got enough money that I haven't had to take out any loans so far to afford my education. I'm definitely grateful for that, and I realize now that all that hassle and work back then was certainly worth it.

▲

Remember that you have to report every scholarship that you receive to the colleges and universities where you apply and to the school that you decide to attend. They will likely lower the amount of your loans as a result, and the fewer loans you have, the better off you are.

☞ ACE YOUR SCHOLARSHIP ESSAY

We won't give you detailed advice on this topic—many great books already do—but here are a few general suggestions from our own experiences:

- Make sure that each essay is customized to the particular scholarship and organization where you're sending it. General essays don't work and they're easy to spot.

- Answer the question. Most scholarship essays will ask that you write on a particular topic or about a particular event. Stick to the instructions.

- Get to know the organization sponsoring each scholarship— what it does, what are its goals and mission. Then tailor your essay to touch on those themes, and describe what role they play in your life. For example, if you're applying for a scholarship from a non-profit organization that supports literacy, talk about why literacy is important and what you've done and will continue to do to promote it. Every organization has an agenda—find out what it is and target your essay appropriately.

- Don't whine. Don't spend your essay talking about how poor you are, how college is too expensive, how you're desperate to find any money, and so on. If you talk about difficulties in your life or your parents' lives, make sure that it's in the context of what you've learned form them.

- Try to sound human. Whoever is reading tons of these scholarship applications needs to find something in your essay that sticks out, that sounds personable and that he or she reader can relate to. Be honest with what you write and with your writing.

- Proofread. You've heard this before, and for a good reason. And don't trust the spellchecker—it can't tell the difference between "their" and "there."

- Follow directions. If the application asks you to put your name and email address on your essay, do it. If there is a word limit, stick to it.

! A WARNING ABOUT SCHOLARSHIP SCAMS

There are many places out there that will let you search large databases of scholarships for those that meet your needs, but you have to be careful. Some of these are not legitimate, and many of them will take your money if you're not careful. You can ask your guidance counselor for suggestions, but if you want to go looking on your own, here a few warning signs that a scholarship or a scholarship search service may not be completely legitimate:

- You have to give credit card or bank account information.

- The application costs money.

- The mailing address is a residential address, rather than a place of business.

- The service guarantees results—no one can guarantee that you'll receive a particular scholarship.

Before you apply for any scholarship you haven't heard of:

- Check with the local Better Business Bureau to make sure there are no complaints filed against the party in question. (Their website is **www.bbb.com**.)

- If the scholarship comes from a national foundation, make sure the foundation exists.

- Check with your school and your guidance counselor to see if anyone has heard of this scholarship or organization.

NAVIGATE THE LOAN MAZE

"The most challenging part about financial aid was understanding what my dad was talking about with fixed rates and subsidized loans and the economics of loans—if I had known those words meant thousands of dollars back then, I would have read up a bit more on what I was getting myself into."

**Recent Grad,
University of Wisconsin - Madison**

Although none of us likes the idea of graduating with a load of debt, two-thirds of undergraduate students take out some type of loan to help them pay for college and, on average, students graduate with about sixteen thousand dollars in debt. This sounds like a lot, and it is, but you should find some comfort in the fact that millions of students just like you have managed to pay back these loans.

There are three general types of loans, outlined below. You should become familiar with them and understand what forms—besides the FAFSA—you'll have to fill out to apply for them. (But as we mentioned, the FAFSA is your first and most important step in the financial aid application process.)

▶ Student Loans

Student loans are either provided or guaranteed by the government and they're the best kind of loans to get because they have extremely low interest rates.

The two most popular student loans are the <u>Stafford Loan</u> and the <u>Perkins Loan</u>.

The Stafford Loan can either be subsidized—the government pays the interest while you're in school—or unsubsidized—you're responsible for the interest, although you can usually defer actually paying it until you graduate. You have to qualify for financial aid in order to receive a subsidized Stafford Loan. As of 2002, the most you could borrow with a Stafford Loan is $2,625 during your freshman year, $3,500 during your sophomore year, and $5,500 for each additional year. Many students choose both the subsidized and unsubsidized loans to get the maximum amount.

Students who demonstrate exceptional financial need receive the Perkins Loan. Your college or university will actually administer this loan, but the funds are provided by the government. This is the best kind of loan that you can get—it's completely subsidized, and the government pays the interest while you're at school and for a 9-month grace period after you graduate. In 2002, you could borrow up to $3,000 per year in Perkins Loans, and you were limited to a total of $15,000.

"Now that I have finished college I can look back and see what I could have done differently. First of all, I would not have taken so many types of loans. Basically, I took whatever they would give me in loans that did not have interest accruing during school. This was a good strategy, but now I have four separate payments to make each month."

Recent Grad,
University of Wisconsin – Oshkosh

Whatever Stafford or Perkins loans you get, the money will go directly to the school each semester. You won't be getting a big fat check from the government or a private organization that's lending you money through the Perkins or Stafford program. In contrast, when you get a scholarship, you'll most likely be receiving a check from the organization sponsoring it—unless it's directly from your college, in which case the scholarship money may be dispersed directly to the bursar's office.

▶ Parent Loan for Undergraduate Students (PLUS)

Your parents can take out the PLUS loan to help pay for your education. They can borrow as much as they need to supplement the financial aid package that you receive, but they can't borrow more than that. This loan is the responsibility of your parents whereas the Stafford and Perkins loans are your responsibility to pay back.

▶ Private Loans

If your family does not receive enough financial aid in the form of Stafford, Perkins, PLUS loans, scholarships, and work-study, your parents might have to apply for additional loans from private lenders. There are many sources for this, but the terms are not as great as those that are provided or supported by the government.

LOOK UNDER EVERY ROCK

There are so many places to find money for college, and you should make sure you consider them all. Big or small,

local or national, you should check into every resource. The billions of dollars given out in financial aid each year can help you pay for college, but they won't come looking for you.

Look everywhere. For example, your parents' employers might offer tuition benefits. The local business owners' association may have a scholarship for students planning to study business. The armed forces offer several options for students, including the Reserve Officer Training Corps (ROTC) program, which pays for tuition, fees, and books, and gives you a monthly allowance in exchange for a service commitment. There are tons of essay contests that are based on a certain topic or a book—even if the particular topic is not one you know a lot about, do some research, read the book, and write the essay.

A great place to visit to check into the many sources of aid for college is **www.finaid.com**. It has clear explanations of every potential source, as well as links to scholarship search engines, specific programs, and government offices.

"I never thought that the local fireman's union would offer a $1,000 scholarship to a graduating senior in our high school...until I got it. I wish I'd checked out more resources rather than just focusing on national scholarships."

**Recent Grad,
Wesleyan University**

DON'T MISS DEADLINES

Can you imagine anything worse than going through all the work of writing essays and filling out applications only to miss a deadline? Everything has a deadline, from the FAFSA to individual scholarship applications. To keep them all straight, write them down on your calendar or in your organizer that you regularly use.

And here's a little cheat technique that we've found works really well—if an application is due on March 1, mark it down as due on February 15 so that you remember to send it out and get it there before the deadline. Every time you learn about a new scholarship that you plan to apply for, mark the due date in your calendar. Make sure that you know whether the due date is when your application must be post-marked or actually received. And never, ever, ever wait until the day before the deadline to submit your application—you never know what might happen to it in the postal service maze.

Deadlines also change from year to year, so don't use last year's due dates thinking they are the same as this year's.

collaborator's corner

▼

A good friend of mine waited until the day of the deadline to begin filling out forms for hundreds of scholarships offered by our school. He was running around all day trying to finish them up, and in the end, he ran to turn them all in at once, but it was five minutes past the deadline and all of his work was for nothing because they weren't accepted.

▲

DON'T RELY ON YOUR PARENTS

"Don't necessarily depend on your parents to do everything for you. I had a friend who got no aid last semester because he thought his dad had filled out all the papers, but his dad had completely forgotten, so he was in a bit of a bind."

Sophomore,
SUNY - Albany

Don't assume that your parents will take care of all of the financial aid forms while you concentrate on filling out the actual college applications. If your parents tell you they will handle it, great, but don't assume that they will without talking to them about it. And even if your parents take on the burden to fill out forms like the FAFSA, looking for and filling out scholarship applications is your responsibility.

SAY THANK YOU

If you win any of the scholarships you apply for, or if you are awarded a scholarship directly from your college, don't forget to say thank you. Find out who is responsible for funding the scholarship—the money has to come from somewhere, after all—and show your gratitude. You may want to write a short letter saying how much you appreciate the financial assistance that a particular scholarship is going to provide to you and mention some of your classes, activities, and future plans, so that the person or group knows what they are making possible.

author's corner

▼

I received a 4-year scholarship from my hometown's Rotary Club. I show my thanks in two ways: I attend a Rotary meeting once a year to let the members of the club know what I've been up to, and to thank them in person for their generosity I also volunteer to help them with one of their annual fundraisers. I figure it's the least I can do, and they appreciate knowing that I don't take the scholarship for granted.

▲

While you're thanking people, don't forget mom and dad. Remember how important their support, both financial and emotional, is to you. You don't want your parents feeling like you're taking them for granted.

making the right decision

Where you choose to go to college depends on a whole set of factors, only one of which is financial aid. For some of us this factor is critically important, for others, not as much. In any case, spend some time understanding each financial aid package that you receive and make sure that you're getting and choosing the best possible deal.

Our main advice at this point is: Don't assume anything and don't give up until you've understood every detail and tried every approach to get as much financial aid as possible.

UNDERSTAND YOUR FINANCIAL AID PACKAGE
▼
COMPARE YOUR OPTIONS
▼
DO SOME RESEARCH
▼
ASK FOR MORE MONEY

UNDERSTAND YOUR FINANCIAL AID PACKAGE

Based on the information in the forms you filled out, which may include the FAFSA, the PROFILE, and any individual school's aid applications, every college where you're accepted will create a financial aid package for you, outlining what your financial aid award will be and where the money will come from. It's frustrating, but each school computes the amount of your financial aid differently.

Many schools will give you financial aid to cover 100% of your need. Some schools may give you less than that. Remember the formula from the previous chapter?

Financial Need=Cost of Attendance–Expected Contribution

Covering 100% of your need means that the school will offer you a combination of loans, work-study, and, hopefully, scholarships equal to the entire amount of your financial need.

There's also a lot of variation in the mix of the financial aid ingredients that each school includes in your package. Some schools will give the majority of aid in the form of loans, others might offer you grants or scholarships. In the next section we'll go through the process of how to compare the financial aid packages you receive, but it's very important that you spend time on each one, together with your parents, to understand what exactly you're being offered.

That single piece of paper outlining your financial aid award that the schools send you can be confusing, but it's really not so bad once you learn how to read it. Here are some suggestions:

- Figure out whether the award you're given is for the whole year or one term. (A $5,000 grant for one year is great; a $5,000 grant for one semester is twice as good.)

- Note how much of the money you're given will have to be paid back. Loans have to be repaid, and with interest; grants and scholarships do not need to be repaid; and work-study means you'll have to work part-time while in school to help fund your education.

- If you're given any loans, make sure you find out the particular terms of your loan, because they vary in factors like repayment procedures and interest rates, as we talked about in the previous chapter.

- Scholarships may also have certain provisions, such as maintaining a particular grade point average. You should understand exactly what these are.

author's corner
▼

If you get a sports or music scholarship, it's important to realize that it may not be valid anymore if something happens that causes you to be unable to participate in the activity any longer. I knew someone who was going to go to college on a lacrosse scholarship, but the summer before he enrolled, he hurt his knee, had to have surgery, and was no longer able to play. He lost the scholarship, could no longer afford to attend the school, and never ended up going back to college.
▲

Many schools will offer to cover 100% of your financial need in the financial aid package, but some will not. If 80% of your financial need is met in your package, this may seem like a lot of money, but it's still only 80% of what you need. This means that you need to come up with the other 20% somewhere else—outside scholarships, loans, savings, etc.

After you spend some time understanding each financial aid package, the final and critical question to ask is: When it comes down to it, how much will you and your parents actually be expected to pay for your college education? Just because a college calculates your need as one value, it does not necessarily mean that you and your family will agree with the assessment. Understanding exactly what you're being offered by each school will help you figure out if you need to find more aid somewhere else and how much you have to come up with.

> *"Getting out of school after four years debt-free and being able to start your professional life knowing everything you make is yours to keep would appeal to anybody, especially me. So as soon as I got my acceptance letter, I ended all thoughts of going to a more expensive college."*
>
> **Junior,**
> **SUNY - Buffalo**

FINANCIAL AID LETTER EXAMPLE

Here's an example of a financial aid award letter—it's very simple, but it gives you a general idea:

Dear Student:

This letter describes your financial aid to attend our college. It supersedes any previous correspondence from our office. Based upon the information we have received, the following is a summary of your financial aid award:

TOTAL COST OF ATTENDANCE	**$ 20,000**
Expected Family Contribution	*$ 9,000*
FINANCIAL NEED	**$ 11,000**
Anticipated State Grant	*$ 3,000*
Memorial Scholarship	*$ 1,000*
Dean's Emergency Fund	*$ 3,000*
Subsidized Stafford Loan	*$ 2,625*
Work Study	*$ 1,375*
TOTAL FINANCIAL AID	**$ 11,000**

Your award is based on the assumption that you will enroll for a minimum of 16 points in the fall semester and 16 points in the spring semester. We also assumed that you will live off campus. Please notify the Office of Financial Aid if you are receiving aid that is not listed above.

Note the fine print in the letter. You must remain a full-time student. This means, should you run into financial or academic trouble mid-semester, you risk losing your financial aid by dropping classes.

COMPARE YOUR OPTIONS

Once you understand each school's financial aid package you should compare your options. Take a deep breath, gather your financial award letters, bring a calculator, and do some math. To make your life a bit easier, at the end of this section we've created a simple template that you can use to do this.

The important thing to keep in mind is not to assume anything or jump to quick conclusions. For example, one school may give you a full tuition scholarship, and this is terrific, but it isn't necessarily as wonderful as it sounds. There are so many other expenses besides tuition, such as room and board, books, transportation, and personal expenses, that tuition costs may not even be half of your total costs. If you have a full tuition scholarship, figure out how much you'll be paying in other expenses.

Many schools also calculate an estimated allowance for transportation and books and personal expenses that are part of the college cost, but their value might not be consistent with your lifestyle. You may end up spending a lot more than estimated, especially if you're buying plane tickets, so you need to calculate your own value for this portion of your college expenses.

You might be surprised to learn that in some cases it might actually end up being cheaper for you to attend a more expensive school than the local or state university if that school offers you a good amount of financial aid. For instance, if a $10,000 school offers you $5,000 in financial aid, and a $30,000 school offers you $26,000, the $30,000 school is actually cheaper. But if $25,000 of the $26,000 is in the form of student loans, then it might not be worth it to you—do you want to be $100,000 in debt when you graduate? It's your call.

It would be nice if we could all get full scholarships and not have to worry about loans, or budgets, or pouring all of our and our family's savings into paying for college. But this rarely happens. As you compare your financial aid options try to weigh all of the factors—how much you want to attend a particular school, how comfortable you are graduating with loans, how your family will be affected by having to pay a significant amount for college, and so on. Weighing these factors will help you pick the right financial aid package, and the right school, for you. The solution might not be ideal, but you can make it work.

COMPARING FINANCIAL AID PACKAGES

You may have your own system, but here's a simple template to help you organize the information as you compare your financial aid packages. Adapt it to your own situation, fill in the amounts, and compare your options.

Total Financial Need (from SAR) =

	School 1	School 2	School 3
Cost of tuition, room, board, fees, personal expenses			
Scholarships/Grants			
Subsidized Stafford			
Unsubsidized Stafford			
Perkins			
Other loans			
Work-study			
Total aid offered			
Total amount you and family will pay (subtract aid from total cost)			

CHOOSING TO STAY LOCAL

by
Laura Gabella
Junior, Orange County Community College

Going to a two-year community college is a lot cheaper than most four-year schools, but many of the experiences are still the same. Making close friends is hard because you're not with them 24-7 like at a four-year school, but it is possible. New friends can be made through sports and other activities. It may seem like that is just like high school again, but it really isn't. At two-year schools, you go more places with groups and thus spend more time with other students than you would in high school.

I think that if you're not 100% sure what you want to do with your life that you should save your money and go to a community college. I know about 7 or 8 people who were going to go away and then decided to go to Orange County Community College instead, who said it was the best decision they made. They were still able to meet new friends and also decide what they wanted to do in life pretty cheaply. You can always transfer to a four-year school later.

And don't worry about running into people from your high school all the time. You see them infrequently unless you purposely have classes together. You can avoid them if you want to!

DO SOME RESEARCH

Before you make the final decision, do a bit of research to figure out how your personal financial aid packages compare to others given out by the schools where you've been accepted.

- Check out the US News and World Report college stats. They usually include the cost of attending each college as well as the average amount of aid that students attending that college receive. Everyone's finances are different, but knowing the average financial aid package can help you figure out where your particular offer stands. It's also good ammunition if you plan to ask for more money (more on this in the next section) and your financial aid award is below the average.

- Ask current students at the colleges you're thinking of attending how much their financial aid awards changed from the first year to the second. It is not unreasonable to think that a college will give freshmen a very attractive financial aid package to get them to attend, and then alter the award the next year.

THE MORE, THE MERRIER

by
Christopher Wipf
Recent Grad, Dartmouth College

Financial aid offices have to brush off complaints every day from applicants who feel that they've been wronged. But if you can send over a copy of a more generous offer from somewhere else, that's quite a bit harder to ignore. My school decided to award me an additional $10,000 per year after seeing what other schools had committed. This made the time and toil of filling out a few extra applications very well spent!

Don't be afraid to lean on your parents. Have them call the school and explain why they don't have money to give you. For example, if your parents sell an investment off which they are going to live, and they thus have an unusually large amount of savings, have them explain the situation to your school.

Never let up on the financial aid department. Make phone calls, write letters, and speak with them in person. The more they know your name and your story, the more they will eventually tire of you and find some aid for you. If they tell you their hands are tied, seek higher help. Ask to talk to bosses of bosses. Persistence will pay off, and someone will eventually be able to help you come up with some money. The first offer they come up with may include loans, but try to hold out for the free money. All schools have special scholarship funds hidden away for special circumstances. Talk to the dean of your school—chances are, he or she has additional funds to help you.

Above all, try to remain professional. Money can become an emotional subject, especially if you find yourself up against a wall. In your letters, phone conversations, and in personal interviews, remain calm and continually state your troubles. Each person has unique circumstances, and the school will be willing to work with you.

ASK FOR MORE MONEY

"After I received all of my acceptances and rejections, I decided that Columbia was the place for me. Unfortunately, they'd given me a package that came to a good deal less than what I'd been offered by my second-choice school. I sent Columbia a copy of the offer, told them the situation, and they were cool enough to match it."

Senior,
Columbia University

If the amount of financial aid that you've received from one or more schools is not enough, or if one school gave you significantly more aid than others, or if the school where you really want to go gave you less aid than a school that's your second or third choice, you should ask for more aid.

We suggest that you write a letter asking for additional financial aid. Even if you also call the financial aid office or make a personal appointment, having your request for aid and the reasons behind it written out in a letter will make it easier for you to communicate them to the financial aid office.

Before you make any contact with the financial aid folks, you need to think about and outline your reasons for asking for more money. "I don't feel like spending all of my savings on paying for college," is not a good reason. "My family has recently had a medical emergency on which a significant portion of our savings was spent," is a good reason. Make a note of any changes in your family's financial situation that reduce the amount of money your family can contribute to your education and outline those in your letter.

A great piece of ammunition in asking for more financial aid is a larger financial aid offer from another college or university. If you have one, mention it in your letter and include a copy.

You should say in your letter how much you want to attend that particular school, how important it is to you, and how you've tried every possible approach to get more money to pay for school—applied to many scholarships, competed in essay contests, saved all of your money from your summer job, etc.

After you mail the letter, call up the financial aid office and if the school is somewhere where you and your parents can visit, ask for an appointment. If you have taken time to come down, they are more likely to take the time to listen to you. When you go, don't wear your best outfit or bring your Prada handbag. Your aid counselor will find it hard to believe that you need more money if you're dressed better than she is.

Keep in mind that even if you do succeed and get more aid from the school for your freshman year, you might not get the same amount of aid the following year. Be ready to fight for it even after you're in college.

Many students are able to squeeze more financial aid from schools after considerable effort, so know that it's not futile. Asking for money can feel embarrassing, but it's not like you're trying to scrounge up for a new stereo.

working for money

It's unavoidable—if you want to pay for college, if you want to have any spending money, and if you want to learn to be responsible for your own finances, you will have to have a job while in college. There are many options that you can choose from, so take some time to figure out the advantages and disadvantages of each one. In this chapter we offer a few tips on looking for a job and getting a job that makes the most sense for you, as well as advice on balancing your job schedule with the rest of your busy college life.

FIND THE RIGHT JOB
▼
BE CREATIVE ABOUT MAKING MONEY
▼
BE A GOOD EMPLOYEE
▼
DON'T OVERWORK YOURSELF

FIND THE RIGHT JOB

"I am glad I got a job when I came to school. It taught me more about the value of what I spend my money on. And having a work schedule made me budget my time better between classes, work, and other activities."

**Junior,
Cornell University**

In an ideal world, you wouldn't have a job while in college. In reality, this almost never happens. You'll most likely have to work at some point, so your goal is to find the job that pays you enough but also doesn't smother you.

Many financial aid offers come with a few thousand dollars worth of work-study. The Federal Work-Study Program makes it easier for students with financial need to work during the school year. If you receive work-study, the government pays a percentage of your paycheck, and this makes you an attractive on-campus employee.

Before you arrive on campus, make sure that you understand how work-study at your school functions. Many schools assign their work-study recipients jobs, but others expect students to find their own. Some schools will require that you work on campus, and others will allow both on- and off-campus work. Some schools expect your paycheck to go straight to the financial aid or bursar office, while others will let students have a paycheck to do what they want with it.

As soon as you get to campus and catch your breath, go to the financial aid office where work-study jobs are usually listed. (There might also be a list in the student employment office at your school.) The earlier you go, the better are your chances of scoring the best jobs—those in the library or other quiet places where you might be able to squeeze in some homework and chill time. Don't be surprised if, as a freshman, you find yourself scraping the bottom of the work-study barrel. Don't let this discourage you, however, because a job cleaning test tubes in a chemistry lab can lead to a job as a student researcher the next year, and a job washing dishes in the dining hall can turn into a job as a student manager.

> *"There are an incredible number of menial jobs on campus. Once you run out of money, you can always get one. It'll be demeaning, horrible, antagonizing, and simply awful. But you'll get paid."*
>
> **Junior,**
> **Cornell University**

If you're not eligible for work-study, as many students are not, you should still have no problem finding a part-time job either on or off campus. Check in with your school's student employment office and see what options are available. If there's a particular place where you'd like to work, say, the art center or the library, go there and see if they're hiring—some jobs never make it to the job listings.

If you can't find a job that you like on campus, check into off-campus opportunities. The local newspaper will probably have listings, and it never hurts to just go to a place and see if they need anyone. Keep in mind, though, that although some off-campus jobs may pay more, they will be less flexible and less understanding when you ask to take time off to finish that midterm paper or study for an exam.

We don't recommend that you have an intensive internship during the school year. But if you're going to work anyway you can check into a few positions that are related to your interests. For example, if you're interested in going into academia after graduation, you might want to intern as a research assistant for one of your professors.

collaborator's corner
▼

Because of circumstances beyond my control, I was unable to turn in my FAFSA on time one year, and I got a much lower financial aid package than normal. As a result, I couldn't afford to go to school. I wasn't about to drop out, but as a last resort, I did end up going part-time. This allowed me to work 40 hours a week to earn money toward tuition costs, while also staying in school and continuing to work toward my degree. It took longer to graduate, but in the end, it was better than the alternative of dropping out.
▲

WE TALK WITH...

Marites Rodriguez
Junior, Northeastern University

Did you participate in a work-study program at your school and, if so, what was your experience like?

I found work-study to be a really great experience. The university provided a list of jobs available, and I was diligent about applying early, so I was able to get a pretty good job. The only downside was that you could only work 20 hours a week, so if I needed more money, I really couldn't get it from that.

On the plus side, it kept me from working more than I should, and everyone I worked with was really understanding about my studies, and that's something I wouldn't have gotten at a regular job.

What was your experience with the cost of dorms? Did you consider outside housing?

I was never at school over the summer, I always went home, and all the apartments involved one-year leases. I didn't want to waste the money on housing I wasn't using, and I didn't want to put myself in the position of trying to find someone to sublet. The dorms were just a lot more convenient. The selection process was really terrible, but when I look at the money I saved, I think it was worth it.

BE CREATIVE ABOUT MAKING MONEY

If you need to pick up some extra cash, consider creating your own job from the skills or talents you possess. You could teach guitar lessons, give massages to the people in your dorm, sell arts and crafts, or tutor. If you're a really fast typist, type up papers for graduate students or professors. If you have a car on campus, offer to take other people with you when you go grocery shopping for a few dollars each. They will appreciate the ride, and you can make enough to cover your gas and perhaps a few dollars extra.

There are also many companies and organizations that want to hire college students during the year to put up posters or write articles or distribute their sample products. Check with the student employment office and find out if your school uses a particular online job listing service, like **www.monstertrak.com**, to let employers advertise these types of jobs.

author's corner
▼

Of course, you could always just do what I did and sign up to write a "Students Helping Students" guidebook. Then you'll earn some money and become a published author! Maybe by the time you read this, they'll be looking for someone to write the next edition of this book.
▲

You're a college student, you're savvy, and you're creative—find a way to use your skills to make some extra cash. Be reasonable, don't do anything illegal, but don't think of a job as something you have to do in an office.

👉 WHAT **NOT** TO DO TO MAKE MONEY

The following are a few ways that real college students tried to earn money and failed miserably. It might sound like it, but we're not making these up. And we're certainly not suggesting that you should attempt any of them.

- Become a clown and perform at children's birthday parties. (Includes buying a costume, shoes, a wig, magic tricks, makeup, balloons, and an air pump.)

- Steal free condoms from the campus health center and sell them to your friends for a quarter apiece. (First, make sure that they're actually free, or else you will be charged for them on the next bill that goes home to your parents. They will not be happy with a $100 bill for condoms—trust us.)

- Go into competition with the campus bookstore by buying people's used textbooks from them at the end of the semester for more than the store is paying and then selling them at the beginning of the semester for less than the store is charging.

- Become an Avon lady. (Includes buying starter kits and extra makeup, and then actually selling them to your friends. Think about this: How many of your college-aged friends actually wear Avon makeup?)

- Ask your classmate if you can borrow his textbooks for the night to study, and then sell his books back to the campus store for cash and tell him you lost them. (When your classmate goes back to the store to re-buy his books, make sure his aren't sitting on the shelves, as he will probably figure out what happened.)

EARNING QUICK CASH

by
Michael Yank
Recent Grad, Harvard University

One way I found to make a decent amount of spending money at college without having to commit to the hours a part-time job demands was to participate in studies run by the various departments of my university. Both the psychology department and business school at my school were always looking for students to help out with their research and paid reasonably for participation.

While this may sound somewhat odd (after all, who wants to be a lab rat?), all the studies were completely harmless and some were even fun. For example, the business school would often run studies involving simple games with prisoner dilemma-style strategizing, and the better you performed in the game, the more money you would receive. Additionally, I was very interested in psychology in college, and participating as a test subject gave me a unique perspective on the way psychologists collect their data.

Of course, my main incentive for doing these studies was the sweet, sweet cash. I found that while most studies offered about $10/hour or less, some studies paid up to $20/hour. As the departments at my school kept pretty busy with research, I could almost always participate in a study whenever I wanted to. While you might not earn as much money as you might working at a job, it's still a fine way to earn a few extra bucks.

BE A GOOD EMPLOYEE

A college job is still a job and you have to treat it somewhat seriously if you want to keep it. Don't show up late for work, dress appropriately, and be generally professional and friendly.

Make an effort to get to know your boss, or at least make sure he or she knows who you are. You may need your boss as a reference for a later job.

If you're a pretty decent employee, your boss may also be more understanding when you ask to cut out early to study for your English midterm or finish your history paper.

DON'T OVERWORK YOURSELF

You need to work and make some money to pay for school, but you also have to make sure that your job doesn't become your primary activity at college.

There's definitely such a thing as working too much, and if you find that your paycheck grows while your grades slide you should reconsider your work schedule. If you're involved in sports, music, clubs, and work, on top of schoolwork, you could burn out by the end of the semester. You especially don't want your grades to suffer, because you could lose your financial aid or lose the chance at receiving future aid. Even if you didn't get much in the way of scholarships your first year, your chances are better the second year if you have proven your ability with strong grades.

Work-study usually allows you to work up to about twenty hours per week, and we suggest that you don't do much more than that. Remember that you can also make money during the summer, when you don't have academic or extracurricular responsibilities, and you can have a full-time job that pays decently.

> "If you want to avoid working during the school year, then during the summer look specifically for a job that pays overtime, and work as much overtime as the company allows."

**Junior,
University of Texas - El Paso**

WORKING YOUR WAY THROUGH COLLEGE

by
Elissa Dunnett
Recent Grad, SUNY - Albany

I never took college seriously until I started paying for it myself. I think the best thing to happen to me academically, personally, and (thus) professionally was my father losing his job and cutting off the tuition and rent payments. I wouldn't change a thing. I had to get a waitressing job quickly to support myself and pay the tuition. Believe me, you take your grades and your education much more seriously when you are the one financing them. Having less time to goof off and slack was really not a bad thing. I actually gave myself time to go out and have fun as well, which was easier to do with my own money. Some people might think that having a job would detract from my studies, but it was quite the opposite—it forced me to learn time and money management skills quickly.

I believe that no matter how much money I may ever make, my own kids will have to work their way through college as well. I'm convinced that you cannot learn to manage something (money, time, your own education) whose value you don't fully understand. In fact, it can't have any value to you if it is handed to you freely. That's why I believe that working to put myself through college was an invaluable experience.

spending wisely

If you think about it, you'll probably be spending money every single day while you're at college. Every time you make a long-distance phone call or eat in the dining hall or do laundry or use your credit card, you are spending money. In order to protect yourself from going overboard and spending exorbitantly, you have to create a budget and stick to it. You also have to be smart about choosing what you spend money on and on what you don't.

Here are some tips and advice on how to make sure that you spend your money wisely and don't spend more than you have.

UNDERSTAND YOUR EXPENSES
▼
SHOP AROUND
▼
TAKE STOCK OF YOUR RESOURCES
▼
CREATE A REALISTIC BUDGET
▼
STICK TO IT
▼
PLAN AHEAD AND SHARE EXPENSES
▼
BE CREATIVE IN CUTTING EXPENSES
▼
TRY TO RESIST (SOME) TEMPTATION

UNDERSTAND YOUR EXPENSES

"You're always going to need more money than the college predicts your average yearly spending will be."

**Sophomore,
SUNY – Albany**

Unless you have unlimited resources—and if you're reading this book, then you probably don't—you'll have to spend your money carefully while at college. And the first thing that you should do is understand exactly what your expenses will be for each year. Do this at the beginning of each school year to make sure that you account for any changes and don't miss any expenses that might later surprise you and your bank account.

Get a piece of paper, grab a calculator, and make a list of your expected expenses for the school year. The first time around you should include every possible expense that you can think of—you'll go through this list later and see if there is anything that you can cut out.

Make sure to include one-time expenses, like purchasing a computer, as well as semester and year-long expenses, like tuition, housing costs, meal plan, telephone service and calls, clothes and books, plane tickets home, movie tickets, and everything and anything that you think you will spend money on. To help you get started, here's a simple template that you can customize and use:

EXPENSE TALLY TEMPLATE

Everyone's situation is different, so make sure that you include every expense that applies to you. The numbers we use here are examples only.

One-Time Expenses		Ongoing Expenses (total $ over the year)	
Computer	$1,000	Tuition	$15,000
Printer	$200	Housing	$4,000
Bedding	$100	Meal Plan	$3,000
Lamp	$40	Books	$2,500
Arm Chair	$100	Cable	$250
Dishes	$50	Parking	$1,200
Shower stuff	$50	Gas	$500
Miscellaneous	$200	Entertainment	$1,000
Plane tickets home	$2,000	Clothes	$500
Trip to Mexico	$2,000	Other personal	$500
Other	$1,000	Other	$1,500
Total	**$6,740**	**Total**	**$29,950**

Grand Total for the Year = $36,690

- We suggest that the first time around, you involve your parents in this exercise. You'll need to be in agreement about who is paying for what—some parents will pay all the necessary expenses and give you extra spending money, while other parents expect you to earn your own way through college. Know who will pay for that frequent late night cappuccino that you buy at the nearby café.

- As you're calculating your expenses, make sure that you're being realistic and practical. Even if you're getting a meal plan, you will definitely eat out or order in once in a while—no human student can handle campus food exclusively for four years!—so include some amount to cover that. If you have a habit or a hobby that you know you can't live without, it's better to plan for it from the beginning than to be surprised later that you're spending so much money.

author's corner
▼

I love to read in my free time, and I love to own all types of books, so I decided ahead of time that whenever I found myself with extra money, I would take a trip to one of the used book stores nearby and spend my time and my money there. This may not seem like a very responsible way to spend money, but it worked for me. It's relaxing, it helps me unwind after class, and it's fun. For me, it's important and definitely worth it.
▲

- Often your school will give you estimates for what you'll be spending on things like books and supplies. That's a good start, but you might want to talk to a few current students to see how much they're actually spending.

- You should also find out if you'll be charged for anything besides tuition and room and board. For instance, most schools will charge separately for phone, cable, and internet connections. If you're living off campus, there may be other expenses like an electric bill or garbage disposal fees that you have to include. If you're thinking of bringing a car to school, find out about parking fees, if there are any. Don't assume what's included—find out exactly how much you'll have to pay.

- Be realistic about what you're bringing with you to college. Many schools will send you a list of "Suggested Items" to buy for your dorm room. Many of these are not really necessary, and you should not spend the money if you don't have to. Think like a minimalist; you can always buy something later should you really need it.

SHOP AROUND

Once you've come up with your list of expenses, you should try to get each of them as low as possible without being unrealistic or overly limiting. The fewer expenses you have, the easier will be your job of paying for college. You won't be able to know every corner that you can cut until you've actually lived on campus for a while, but there are a few things to think about in advance.

Look at each item on your list of expenses and ask yourself if you can't lower the cost somehow. For instance, find out from your college what the rates are for the campus contracted phone company. If you're allowed to switch companies, find one with better rates. Or, if it will be cheaper, just use phone cards. If you have a cell phone, ask yourself if a ground line is really even necessary at all. Why pay monthly charges for both phones if one will be sufficient?

As far as a meal plan goes, don't pretend that you will eat three meals a day seven days a week just to please your parents—if you know you will sleep through breakfast every day, then don't get the full meal plan. It's just plain silly to pay for more meals than you're eating. You might be able to save even more money if you have a kitchen available to you in your apartment or dorm and you decide to buy groceries and do your own cooking.

> *"Since I had my own kitchen, it was cheaper for me to be off the meal plan and cook my own food."*
>
> **Sophomore,**
> **New York University**

Check with your school to find out if a mini-fridge comes with your dorm room. Some schools will provide them for free, others will ask you to rent one. If your room doesn't come with a fridge, you may want to consider purchasing one rather than renting. The prices to purchase are not much more than the rental prices, especially if you're going to use it for multiple years. You may also be able to purchase a used fridge from a college student who is moving out of the dorms and no longer wants a fridge that is only a few years old.

If you're thinking about buying a computer for your room, know that this isn't something that you have to do. We admit, it's definitely more convenient, but if you need the extra cash then this is one place to find it. Consider what you'll be using your computer for: If you're only going to be using it to check your email and write a paper now and then, you could probably just use the public computer labs. But if you're planning on majoring in computer science, a personal computer might be a good idea. Get to know the available computer facilities at your school and make a decision you can live with.

With all items that you're buying for school, remember that you don't need to have new ones. Go to local garage sales, shop around on eBay, check out your local thrift stores, and see what you can bring from home. College is definitely not the time to invest in nice stuff—you need something that's usable and something you can live with, but living in style can wait a few years. And when it comes to books and textbooks, definitely try to find used ones— they are so much cheaper and sometimes the important parts are already highlighted for you, which can be quite helpful. You can easily find used books at your college store or online, at websites like **www.varsitybooks.com**.

One final suggestion: Do your research. This is your and your family's money and you have to squeeze as much out of it as you can. Don't just assume that living off campus is cheaper than living in the dorms, for example.

collaborator's corner
▾

I thought living off campus would be a lot cheaper, since in New York, the dorms are really expensive and I had to buy a meal plan that I knew I'd never use. What I didn't count on were the high housing costs in a large city as compared to a small city. My friends back home were paying $300 a month, while my rent was $1000. Another thing was that when you move to a big city, you usually have to use a broker to get an apartment. I've moved twice in New York, both times paying $1500 in broker's fees!
▲

LIVING OFF CAMPUS

by
Luke Donahue
Recent Grad, University of Minnesota - Duluth

Having lived both on and off campus, I thought I'd offer some on- vs. off-campus living advice to other students. A lot of factors go into the decision about which option is best, and monthly rent is just one of them.

Most schools have mandatory meal plans for on-campus housing. Remember that if you'll have a meal plan, it's unrealistic to assume that you will not eat anywhere else. You will still keep food in your dorm to snack on and this will cost money. Similarly, for off-campus living, you should be realistic about how often you will make food at home and how often you will eat out.

It's also easy to forget that there are some off-campus costs that are included in the price of dorm living. Typically, electricity, heat, and basic phone service are a part of your dorm payment. However, in apartments, some or all of these expenses can be extra, so make sure you're clear about these costs and factor them into your plans.

Your proximity to campus can be an issue when figuring the costs of living on or off campus. If you have to drive to school or take public transportation, the small daily costs can quickly add up.

Remember to consider the specifics of each arrangement and figure out the best fit for your financial situation and personal preferences.

TAKE STOCK OF YOUR RESOURCES

The next step after you've thought about your expenses is to figure out where you'll get the money to pay for them. You have some savings, your parents may be paying for some things, and you've gotten a few scholarships, loans, and a work-study allowance. Make a list of all of the sources of money that you'll have during the year—you'll use this list in the next section to create a budget.

As with your expenses, be realistic and get some input from your parents. If you have $2,000 in your savings account but are planning to take a summer trip before college, don't put the entire $2,000 as available savings.

Here's a simple template to get your organized—create a similar one for yourself and fill in the appropriate numbers:

Personal Savings	$3,000
Parents' Contribution	$10,000
Scholarship 1	$5,000
Scholarship 2	$7,000
Loan 1	$2,625
Loan 2	$3,000
Work-study Allowance	$4,200
TOTAL	**$34,825**

BUDGETING WISELY

by
Lisa Nortman
Recent Grad, Winona State University

When I first arrived on campus, it seamed like everyone was trying to pawn something off on me. It was as if they could smell that I was armed with a bank account holding my precious earnings from my summer job. I thought that surely with my earnings, I was ready to live the high life in college. There were parties that offered unlimited refills of beer when you bought the cup for $5.00 (of which you would only to be able to get one full glass before the keg runs out). Then there were the trips to the mall, the weekend getaways with my newfound friends, and, of course, the endless supply of late night pizza, which found my dorm room courtesy of a friendly pizza delivery boy.

One problem you will definitely not have in college is finding a place to spend your money. But you can definitely find ways to have a great time and not empty your bank account. The most important thing you can do is budget your money! Budget, budget, budget! If you learn nothing else, learn how to budget. You don't need to have spreadsheets accounting for every little cent, but you do need to have some kind of idea of where your money goes. How many times have you asked yourself, "Where did all my money go?" If you simply keep track of where you spend your money, and on what, you will have no problem keeping track of your funds.

Also, if you allow yourself a weekly allowance, say $30.00, you will be able to avoid temptation better because you'll know your limits. A sale at the Gap, as exciting as it may be, is not as important as buying textbooks. You need to prioritize and realize that in college, things like books come before clothes.

CREATE A REALISTIC BUDGET

The word "budget" sounds really official, but really it's just an account of your expenses and the resources that you'll have to cover those expenses over a period of time. Since you don't have unlimited resources, you need to stick to a budget—this means that you'll have to watch what you spend, and make sure that you don't spend any more money than you actually have coming in during that period.

Since you've already estimated your expenses and your available resources, creating a budget should be easy. Start with figuring out your budget for the entire year, and then you can do this month by month.

The first thing to do is to take the two components—your expenses and resources—and compare them. On the next page is an example of how you might want to do this.

 **ANNUAL BUDGET EXAMPLE**

Expenses		Resources	
One-time total	$6,740		
Tuition	$15,000	Savings	$3,000
Housing	$4,000	Parents' Contribution	$10,000
Meal Plan	$3,000	Scholarship 1	$5,000
Books	$2,500	Scholarship 2	$7,000
Cable	$480	Loan 1	$2,625
Parking	$1,200	Loan 2	$3,000
Gas	$500	Work-study	$4,200
Entertainment	$1,000		
Clothes	$500		
Other personal	$500		
TOTAL	**$35,420**	**TOTAL**	**$34,825**

In this example, using the numbers we've pulled out of the air, there's a total shortfall of $595. This means that you need to find a way to either increase your resources by that amount—perhaps by working extra hours during the summer—or to reduce your expenses—by not getting cable, leaving the car at home, or reducing the amount of money you spend on clothes, as a few examples.

If your budget comes out even or, even better, if you end up with more resources than expenses, great. If not, then you need to go back through the expenses that you've estimated and see if there's anything that you can reduce. If you find that your expenses are pretty accurate, then think about ways to increase your resources—you may have to get an extra job during the summer or you could ask if your parents could contribute more to your education.

You don't have to make your expenses and your available resources exactly the same, but they should come relatively close. As the year progresses, you'll probably adjust your budget as you find that you're spending more or less on certain things—it's hard to know exactly that far in advance. Think of your budget as a guideline, but understand that you'll have to be flexible and figure out month by month how to make it work.

After you create your budget for the year, it makes sense to create a monthly budget that will tell you approximately how much money you can spend. As with your budget for the year, try to be as realistic as possible. On the next page we've included a simple template to help you get organized—you'll notice that it's very similar to the annual budget template.

Once you have a budget, the key is to use it! Keep track of your expenses every month, at least as you get used to managing your own money. Write them down on a piece of paper or use a spreadsheet program, but do write them down. It's easy to think that you can keep track of your spending in your head, but things do tend to slip through. If you get into the groove of writing down what you spend and knowing when you've reached your limit, you'll be much better off!

MONTHLY BUDGET TEMPLATE

In most cases, you'll pay tuition and room and board once every semester, so we won't include these expenses in the monthly budget. You should know, from your annual budget, how much money you have to save during the year and each month to pay for your share of tuition and room and board, so we've included that as an expense in the monthly budget—you should think of it that way and put that amount of money in the bank each month.

Expenses		Resources	
Savings Contribution		Work Study	
Books/School Supplies		Savings Account	
Meals (if not already paid in meal plan)		Other	
Take-out/Going out			
Car Expenses			
Other Travel Expenses			
Phone/Internet			

As you keep track of your monthly expenses, it might help to stick to the same categories you created in your budget—so a meal out would go into the Take-out/Going Out category.

WE TALK WITH...

Megan Hutchin
Sophomore, Middlebury College

How did you arrange purchasing items for your dorm/apartment with your roommate so you shared expenses evenly?

My roommate and I talked over the phone before we moved in, as to who was bringing what in terms of big stuff that you just don't need two of in a little room. I brought the printer, she brought the stereo. When we got to school we went out and bought a rug together. I would suggest that you don't share costs on stuff because then it makes it harder to divide up at the end of the year. We ended up throwing the rug out because it had gotten so dirty, but we each went home with our own stuff.

What was your agreement with your roommate about groceries and other common expenses?

My roommate and I didn't have to buy groceries, but in terms of common expenses, we just kind of had an "it'll all work out in the end" mentality. If I bought a printer cartridge for our printer, she bought paper for the next couple of weeks. Other people might find it easier to figure out a strict split of costs, but our system worked well for us and never caused any problems.

Did you ever have to find a creative way of making your roommate pay up when she owed money for something?

I'm not good at this stuff, so generally I just let it go or just hinted it at being broke and other people owing me money, hoping she would catch on. Generally though, I never had this problem and I would say that it's better just to ask right out.

STICK TO IT

As we've learned, sometimes very painfully, the harder part is not creating a budget, but sticking to it. We've been preaching about this budget stuff for pages now, so let us just offer you a few quick thoughts:

- If you stick to your budget and save diligently, you will not only avoid getting into trouble and significant debt, but you might find yourself graduating with a nice cushion to get you through the very stressful first months of "How am I going to pay for rent without a job!?"

"Every penny I made during college and during the summers between semesters went towards paying for school. I didn't have much left for extra expenses, but was able to save up about $2,000 from my summer internship before my senior year. Wow, did that help during the first few weeks in New York, with the paychecks from my job not yet coming and rent, moving, and food expenses piling up."

**Recent Grad,
Wesleyan University**

- Think about your budget kind of like a game that you need to win: Every month you want to end up spending less than your limit.

- Learning how to live on a budget is useful in college, but it's one thousand times more useful after you graduate. If you envy some of your classmates because they don't have to worry about paying for college, they might envy you after graduation when you can manage your finances.

PLAN AHEAD AND SHARE EXPENSES

You can usually save lots of money just by doing a little planning. For example, you know when you'll likely be going home for vacations, so buy your plane and bus tickets in advance. Use the Internet to compare prices and get the best deals on travel, and always keep an eye out for specials deals. When you decide which classes to take, go to the bookstore and search for used textbooks—they're usually the first to go.

If you have roommates or housemates, sharing expenses can save you a lot of money. It can also cause a lot of problems, so you have to be smart about it.

Splitting regular expenses, such as electric bills, is a good strategy. Talk to your roommate or roommates and figure out how you will actually handle this—will each of you pay half of the bill or will you alternate paying entire bills, for example.

However, things get trickier when you start splitting costs for items that you actually buy, such as a fridge or a TV, because you'll run into the problem of figuring out who gets to keep what when you move out. There are two ways to solve this:

- One person can just buy the whole item, and then take it when he or she moves out, or;

- You can split the cost of the item, and agree ahead of time which one of you will get to take the item at the end of the year. This person can, when he or she moves out, pay the others a percentage of what was originally paid. For instance, if you have two roommates, you each pay $50 for a $150 fridge. After a year when you all move out, whoever is keeping the fridge pays each of the other two $25, so that he ends up paying only $100 for the fridge, and the other two people get to use it for the year for only $25. As long as you all agree ahead of time on an arrangement, you should be able to avoid many arguments about what belongs to whom.

Another situation you might encounter is a roommate who comes from a very different financial background than you. Maybe your roommate's parents pay the entire tuition and give him or her lots of spending money. Your roommate may be constantly encouraging you to spend money on take-out food or wanting to go shopping. Or, you might have a roommate who wants to make all sorts of dorm/apartment improvements—flat screen television, custom made bookshelves, new stereo system. These are all things that would be great, and your roommate may suggest that it's cheaper for you two to split the costs.

How to deal with expensive roommates? The best way is to be honest and upfront from the beginning. When you first move in, make it clear that you are on a fixed income, and that if you want to stay in school, you are going to have to be frugal. You don't have to make a formal declaration, but find a way to slip it in. Then stick to it. Even if your roommate pressures you to order delivery, be strong and go swallow that dining room food that you've already paid for. Surely you're not always going to say no—and you shouldn't—but develop the habit early so that your roommate won't expect you to join him or her every time.

You should also be prepared to deal with having a roommate who takes your stuff or eats your food. Maybe it's your clean socks or your cereal or your printer paper, but even the small things can add up. You don't want to be a nag and might want to just let it go. But a better approach, if this truly becomes a habit, is to mention it to your roommate in a friendly way coupled with a suggestion: "Hey, since you love that cereal so much, could you pick us up an extra box the next time you're at the store?" Be subtle, but be firm.

BE CREATIVE IN CUTTING EXPENSES

"I set a mental budget for myself and also passed on going out with friends every once in a while. Plus, there are tons of cheap and even free things for students to do while at college, you just have to dig a bit to find them and be creative."

**Recent Grad,
Winona State University**

There are tons of things to do at college that don't cost much at all, and shopping at thrift stores is more fun than it is trying to cut down on purchases. As you go through the year, stick to your budget and try to find ways to cut some corners without cutting out the essentials.

Here are a few ideas:

- Buy non-perishable goods, like pasta or cereal or paper towels, in bulk. If you're worried about storage space, keep them back home and bring small quantities to school that you can replenish over breaks.

- Instead of using the phone all the time, write emails and Instant Messenger with your friends and family.

- Bring a bike to campus to get around, or walk; it's cheaper than taking the bus or having a car. (But if you do decide to ride the bus, buy a bus pass for the semester or the year if it will save you money on fares.)

- Instead of taking the bus or train home, find someone who lives near your hometown, or who has to drive past your town, and carpool with him or her, splitting the cost of the gas.

- Shop off campus for food and other goods—on-campus stores tend to be more expensive.

- Save scrap paper to write notes on or print rough drafts.

- Try to avoid bars. Instead, go to parties where drinks are provided by the host, and the social scene can be more fun.

- Clip coupons and buy things that are on sale.

- Don't get 3-way calling or call waiting for your phone unless you really need them—they can add up to a lot on your monthly bill.

- Don't open any packaged books until you're absolutely sure you're taking the class. Once you open them, you often can't return them.

TRY TO RESIST (SOME) TEMPTATION

"Don't go to the grocery store unless you really need something and have a list—not when you're bored or hungry."

**Junior,
Wittenberg University**

It may be hard to do, and you might never have had to do this before, but if you want to keep yourself financially stable, you have to resist the urge to buy everything you see. We're definitely not going to suggest that you deny yourself every single meal out with friends or never buy new clothes or skip every spring break in Mexico. That's unrealistic and unnecessary. You don't need to save every penny in college just for the sake of saving money and building up your bank account—you just need to manage your expenses to make sure that you have enough money to cover the things you absolutely must pay for, like tuition.

collaborator's corner
▼
Avoiding temptation turned out to be a bit difficult for me. When I moved to New York, I found myself "needing" everything. Most of my friends had a lot more money than I did, and I found myself shopping at some of the best stores in New York, thinking I needed things because I couldn't get them back home. By the time summer was over, it was often hard to scrape together the money for the items that I really did need. So don't overlook this step. Put money for rent and necessary items aside in your savings account and then go shopping with the leftover

money in your checking account. But try to control yourself if you can, and remember that if you save it now, it will be there later when you truly do need it.

▲

There's no science to determining which temptation you should resist and which you should give into. One way to think about it is that if something is really important to you and would make you really happy to have, you should get it, but if it's something you could live without, then perhaps skip it this one time.

"It's really easy to go through a hundred dollars a weekend in college. Many of us start out spending too much money, only to realize that when the bank account is suddenly empty. Realize that while you'll have many expensive fun opportunities in the first few months of school, they'll still be there later in the year and in the years after that. There's no need to do everything right away."

**Freshman,
Emory University**

author's corner

▼

I have two little tricks I use to keep myself from buying too much. I was a janitor in a middle school for three summers in a row, so when I see something I really like, I ask myself "How many hours would I have to scrape gum and graffiti off desks in order to earn the money to pay for this?" It really puts things in perspective. If I decide it's worth it, I'll go home and sleep on it for a night. If I'm still thinking about it the next day, then I'll go back and buy it. This wait

keeps me from impulsively buying the things that I don't
really care that much about.
▲

And try to avoid expensive habits as well, such as smoking, drugs, or gambling. This will save you tons of money.

> *"It's better to not have any habits to feed—my friends who chain-smoke are basically throwing money down the drain."*

> **Junior,**
> **Wittenberg University**

saving wisely

A major part of being responsible is realizing that you'll have to save at least some portion of the money that you make for future expenses, and the sooner you start, the better off you'll be. It's true now, and it's true after you graduate. You should pay the expenses you can't avoid, spend a few bucks on things that make you happy, but always try to save at least a portion of your paycheck each month.

Here are some tips on how to go about it.

OPEN A BANK ACCOUNT
▼
SAVE FOR EMERGENCIES
▼
CONSIDER DIRECT DEPOSIT
▼
KEEP RECORDS AND RECEIPTS

OPEN A BANK ACCOUNT

The best way to save your money is in a bank account. You'll be much less tempted to spend it if it's not hanging around in your room or luring you from your wallet, and you'll earn some interest. You may want to open up two accounts—one savings and one checking—since they serve two different purposes. Your savings account can hold your spending money that you can withdraw from the ATM, emergency funds, holiday spending money, and any other savings. More immediate funds that you need to pay bills should be in your checking account. Checking accounts don't pay interest; savings accounts do.

Take some time to find the best bank for your needs. You'll probably want to choose a bank that has a branch near your college, so you have easy and convenient access to your money when you need it. It's also important that you can easily get to your bank's ATM machine to withdraw or deposit cash or checks—you don't want to be dealing with long lines and inconvenient hours. And using ATMs that belong to other banks can get expensive since most will charge you a one- or two-dollar fee, in addition to another one- or two-dollar fee that your own bank will charge.

"Shop around for the best bank and open an account with one that's on campus because it's a lot more convenient. If there is no bank on campus, open an account with a bank that has an ATM on campus, so you don't get charged every time you want to use the ATM."

**Sophomore,
SUNY – Albany**

Besides location of the bank and its ATMs, there are a few other things you need to consider. Here's a checklist that can help you figure out which bank to choose:

✓ Can you access your account via the Internet?

✓ What is the minimum balance that you have to maintain to avoid incurring fees? Most banks will require you to keep a certain amount of dollars in your account, and you should try to find one where that required amount is low, perhaps a few hundred dollars. You never know what you'll need the money for and you want to avoid paying extra fees.

✓ Are there any kinds of monthly fees for either your savings or checking account? Some banks will have these, but there are plenty that don't—find one.

✓ How many checks can you write per month without incurring extra fees? For some banks this number will be as low as five per month, for others, twenty-five. While you won't be writing dozens of checks every month, make sure that you have enough leeway not to incur fees.

✓ Do you get your first set of checks for free? You should, unless you want some kind of a personal design, which you really don't need.

✓ Can you get an ATM card that's also a debit card? We'll talk more about debit cards in the next chapter, but if you can combine your ATM with your debit card, it's much more convenient.

✓ What type of overdraft protection service is available? If you write a check for an amount that's more than what you have in your account, it will bounce and you'll be charged twenty or thirty dollars, depending on your bank. Some banks offer an overdraft protection service, which advances you a few hundred dollars to cover the check, and that you then have to pay back promptly.

✓ Does your bank have a local branch in your hometown? You'll want to access your money when you go home, and if you can keep it all in one place, it will be easier.

Also check with your school—some make special deals with local banks for student accounts, and you might be able to save some money on checks or avoid a minimum balance charge.

In order to open a bank account, you'll need several forms of ID, as well as proof of address. Some banks also offer discounts or special gifts to college students, so make sure you tell the bank you're a student.

SAVE FOR EMERGENCIES

The whole idea behind emergencies is that we don't know when they're going to occur. We can't plan for them, but we can save for them. Make sure you put a little of your money away with each paycheck just in case an emergency comes up. This could be anything from a medical emergency, to car troubles, to an unexpected trip home. You don't know what it's going to be, and you don't know how much you'll need, but every little bit will help, so start saving now.

Decide on a reasonable amount and make sure to put it away every month. Hopefully you'll never have a major emergency, but you'll have a savings cushion you could later spend on a vacation or to pay rent on your first apartment after graduation.

CONSIDER DIRECT DEPOSIT

If you have a job during the school year, consider setting it up so that your paycheck will be deposited directly into your bank account. This is great for many reasons: You don't have to pick up your check and manually deposit it, and you'll be less tempted to spend the money if it just goes directly to the bank.

If you opt against direct deposit, then at the very least, don't cash your whole paycheck when you go to the bank. Deposit most of it, and only keep an amount of cash that you think you'll spend in the course of a week.

Banks like direct deposit—they save money by not having to process a bunch of paper—and they might give you a deal if you set it up. Make sure to ask.

author's corner
▼
At my bank, I have direct deposit of my paycheck set up and, because of this, I have no minimum balance. This means that I don't end up paying finance charges for having too low a balance in my account. This was one of the main reasons I chose to do business with this bank when I was a new student.
▲

KEEP RECORDS AND RECEIPTS

Always, always, always keep a record of the money you deposit and take out of your bank account. Whenever you write a check or use your debit card, write it down in your checkbook, and make sure the book stays balanced. Get into the habit of saving bank statements, bills, tax forms, receipts, and any other financial papers for your records. You can buy a cheap filing cabinet at an office supply store to help you stay organized. Or, even just having a folder where you put financial papers is better than leaving them scattered on your desk and floor, or crumpled up in your jeans pocket.

If you don't get in the habit of tracking your checks and debit card expenses, you'll never know how much you have in your bank account, and it will be harder to realize how much you're spending. The next thing you know, you'll be down to zero, and sorry for not being wiser about watching your expenses. Or worse, you'll write a check and not have enough money to cover it, and get stuck with an overdraft charge of twenty bucks or more.

Although it doesn't happen often, banks do make mistakes. And unfortunately, they rarely make the mistake of depositing a million dollars in your bank account. Keeping records will allow you to catch any mistakes, such as uncredited deposits.

staying out of debt

One of the easiest things to do, without even realizing that you're doing it, is to spend money that you don't have on things that you don't really need and get yourself into a huge amount of debt that takes years to pay off. You may be extremely mature and careful with your money and never get into this situation, but it pays to always be on guard.

It's a lot easier to get into debt than you think, particularly credit card debt. The reason we know this is because we've all been there to one degree or another. In fact, thousands of students each year graduate from college with huge credit card debts.

This doesn't have to happen to you, and here are some suggestions for how to avoid this unpleasant and expensive situation.

UNDERSTAND CREDIT CARDS
▼
BE SMART WITH CREDIT
▼
MAKE ALL PAYMENTS ON TIME
▼
KNOW WHEN TO GET HELP

UNDERSTAND CREDIT CARDS

Before we dive into talking about the good and bad sides of credit cards, let's get the basics down about what credit cards are, how they work, and what features different credit cards have.

There are three major types of cards that all get called credit cards:

▶ **Credit Card:** A card that lets you make purchases and then allows you to either pay the entire amount of what you've spent in a given month, or just a portion of that amount, with the rest to be paid later, with interest.

▶ **Charge Card:** A card that lets you make purchases like a credit card but requires that you pay the entire bill in full at the end of the month. In other words, you can't shift your balance and pay some now and some later.

▶ **Debit Card (or Check Card):** A card that's linked to your bank account and that allows you to make purchases without using cash. Every time you make a purchase, the amount of the purchase is deducted from your bank account and you can't charge more on the card than you have in your account. Debit cards are accepted wherever you see the logo featured on the card—if it's a MasterCard, then you can use it wherever you see the MasterCard Logo.

Beyond these distinctions, each credit card comes with a particular set of features and fees, and it's important that you know what they are and how they affect you. Check out our table on the next page to get an idea of the main things you should check about each credit card you're considering.

CREDIT CARD FEATURES

Annual Percentage Rate (APR)	This is the interest rate that will be charged to any balance that you revolve on your card—i.e., if you don't pay your monthly balance in full, a % will be added to the revolving balance when your bill comes the next month, and so on.	You want your APR to be as low as possible. Be especially careful because often credit card companies will give you a low APR for the first several months, and then hike it after that.
Annual Fee	An annual membership fee.	You can definitely get a credit card in college without a membership fee.
Grace Period	The number of days you have after the end of one payment period to pay your balance in full and avoid interest charges on new purchases that you made.	25 days is standard and you shouldn't get a card that's less than that.
Late Payment Fee	Amount you'll get charged, on top of any interest charges, if your payment is late.	Usually around $20-$25.
Incentives	Most cards come with incentives. For each dollar you spend you might get frequent flyer miles, free phone minutes, or just dollars that you can spend on whatever you want.	You can usually get a bonus for getting a card for the first time—such as 10,000 frequent flyer miles.

BE SMART WITH CREDIT

Misusing credit cards is probably one of the most common ways that college students get themselves into financial trouble, so think twice before signing up for one. You'll be approached by dozens of credit card companies on campus and through the mail, offering you what might be your first ever credit card with no annual fee, low interest rate, and a cool gift like a hat or a funky pen. Being wanted is good, but you should understand why you're so wanted. Unfortunately, it's not because you're smart or good-looking or can speak backwards. Credit card companies want you to sign up now, when you're a college student, because they think that they'll get to keep you—and your business—for a long time after you graduate. And they're not wrong—many people do keep the same credit cards after they graduate.

You have to resist the temptation to sign up for the first card that you're offered or to get the one that comes with the coolest gift. Take some time, do some research, and figure out which one is best for you. Credit card companies aren't your parents—they don't offer you something because it's good for you. They offer you something because it's good for them. Check out the features of each card, make sure that you understand what the interest rate is and if it will increase in a few months, and make your decision.

"Get a credit card that you, not your parents, pay for, and don't let your card carry a balance. This way, you'll have a record of all your purchases, you'll learn the value of money by paying your bill yourself, and, if you pay your whole bill right away, you won't pay any money in interest. Plus, you'll

build a good credit history for which you'll be thankful."

**Senior,
George Mason University**

Here are our suggestions for which credit card to get and how to use it:

- Don't get more than one card. Having more than one card doesn't make you more adult or more sophisticated; it increases the risk that you'll spend more money than you have.

- Don't sign up for a card over the phone. You've probably heard the horror stories about people being scammed over the phone and giving away personal information—you don't want to end up in that situation.

- You should never pay a fee for a credit card. If you didn't pay a fee initially but notice it on your statement, call the company right away and tell them that you want to cancel your card. They will likely remove the fee rather than lose your business.

- Consider getting a debit card instead of a credit card. That way, you can't possibly get into debt or credit trouble because you can't spend more than what you have in your bank account.

- Get a low line of credit to begin with. The company might offer you several thousand dollars in available credit, but you should start with $500 or $1,000 at the high end. That way you'll avoid purchasing too much with your card. If you get a credit card with a high credit line, call them up and ask for a reduction. You can always increase it later.

- Once you have your card, try to pay as much of your balance as you can each month and establish a goal for yourself to pay the balance in full. If you just make the minimum payment, you'll end up paying a lot more in interest.

- If you know that your payment is going to be late, call the credit card company. They may extend your grace period or offer you another arrangement. Be proactive.

- Don't use your credit card to pay your tuition bill. It's asking for trouble. First of all, you'll have to pay interest on it, and, second of all, many schools are beginning to use outside companies to validate credit cards, charging a "convenience fee." If the tuition due date comes and you don't have the money, rather than putting in on the plastic, check into your school's financing programs to postpone payments. There might also be fees associated with this, but they will be a lot less than the interest that credit card companies will charge you.

If you think you're smarter than the average student and that you can't possibly end up in debt, think about this: A recent study by college lender Nellie Mae found that college students carry an average credit card balance of $2,327, and one in five has a high-level balance between $3,000 and $7,000. This may not sound so bad, but if you pay only $100 per month on a $3,000 credit card bill at an 18% interest rate, it will end up costing you over $4,000 and take more than three years!

Be smarter than this!

collaborator's corner

▼

I managed to get myself into credit card debt; it was simply something that was unavoidable because I couldn't get money anywhere else. I found myself with three separate cards, all carrying balances and high interest rates. At this point, the smartest thing I did was to get a new credit card that had free balance transfers, and offered a really great interest rate for those transfers for the first few months. As soon as the three cards were all transferred to one, I cut up the old cards so I wasn't tempted to use them again, and I immediately worked toward paying down the one with the huge balance. The lower interest rate really saved me some money in the end.

▲

! THE BEAUTY AND THE BEAST OF CREDIT

Credit cards aren't inherently bad and they provide a ton of convenience and ways to get free stuff if you use them right. But they can easily get you in debt trouble as well. Here are a few of the pros and cons of credit cards as food for your thoughts.

PROS

- Credit cards are convenient and you don't have to worry about always having cash in your wallet.

- Credit cards are safer than cash—if yours is stolen, and you report it, you're only responsible for up to fifty dollars of what is charged on it after it's out of your hands.

- Credit cards help you get your credit history started, which can be helpful when you graduate.

- If you have an emergency—like you have to fly home on short notice—credit cards offer you a way to pay for it even if you don't have enough money in your bank account at the time.

CONS

- Being able to buy stuff without actually paying for it with cash can be tempting and you might spend more than you're able to afford.

- If you have a large credit limit, you might start thinking that you actually have that amount of money to spend, when in reality you only have what's in your bank account.

- If you revolve your balance, interest payments will grow and become considerable.

- If you don't pay your credit card bills on time, your credit history will be negatively affected, making it harder for you to get any type of credit, like a car loan, later on.

MAKE ALL PAYMENTS ON TIME

You will have bills for credit cards, student loans, utilities, rent, tuition, insurance, car payments, and any number of other expenses. Make it a habit to pay these bills on time. There are often extra charges for late or skipped payments, which is the last thing you need. Not to mention that making payments on time will help you build a good credit history, which will be important for borrowing money in the future.

When you get any bill, write the date when you have to send the payment—rather than the actual due date—in your organizer. Consider paying bills online directly from your bank account. Most banks offer this feature and it's really convenient and saves you the cost of a stamp. It also allows you to schedule payments to go out on a certain date, which, if you have trouble remembering to do this yourself, is helpful.

Let's face it: You may accidentally miss a payment once in a while. Or maybe you just don't have the money at some point. As soon as you know you won't be making your payment on time, call the creditor to make other arrangements. Explain your situation and tell them when you think you can make the payment. Chances are they will understand at least once, and will often waive any fees for a late payment.

KNOW WHEN TO GET HELP

If you do get into debt and find your credit card balance growing every month, get some help. Waiting and hoping that it will go away doesn't work—we've all tried it.

Talk to your parents and seek their advice. No, it's not fun to admit that you made a mistake and you're almost guaranteed a lecture, but they can be very helpful and most will be understanding. Remember, they deal with things like bills and credit cards all the time, and they've probably been in a bind or two during their lives as well.

You can also speak to a financial counselor at your school and see what solutions he or she can offer.

There are many non-profit organizations that can help you reduce your credit card debt. They will negotiate with your creditors on your behalf, help to consolidate your debt if it's on multiple cards, and will also lower the interest rate that you're paying. The National Foundation for Credit Counseling is one of the largest ones, and they have a helpful website you can start with, **www.debtadvice.org**.

You're not bad or stupid for getting into credit card debt, and no one is going to pass judgment on you based on that. Instead of trying to figure out how to deal with it on your own, get some advice from your parents, your school, and debt professionals.

the daily grind

Budget, loans, credit card payments, financial aid forms...it can all get overwhelming. We wish we could take it all off your hands—but that wouldn't do you much good in the long run, since you have to learn to do all this responsible money stuff at some point.

What we can offer are some pieces of advice from our own experiences and some things to focus on as you figure out the best way to go to college, pay for it, and graduate without being completely broke.

▶ HAVE FUN, BE FRUGAL

Being frugal doesn't mean that you lead a drab life void of any pleasure. As a college student you're surrounded by tons of fun, entertaining, and enjoyable things that you can do for free or on the cheap. Parties, movies, rallies, sports, theater, friends, clubs—just look around and recognize how many awesome things you could be doing without paying more than a few dollars for them. If your campus is in a bustling city filled with opportunities to spend tons of money, don't forget that you could be doing fun things on campus, and saving tons of money instead.

▶ TAKE ADVANTAGE OF YOUR INDEPENDENCE

This is probably the first time you've really had to handle your own money and be responsible for your education and, at least in part, for paying for it. That's pretty great if you think about it. You'll make mistakes and you'll get yourself in a bind a few times, but you'll be doing this on your own and you'll learn some valuable skills as you go along. You'll also have a great opportunity to practice for the real world after graduation. And trust us, it helps.

> *"My parents paid for my entire tuition, and although it was extremely helpful, sometimes I actually do regret it. Overall, my peers who put themselves through college have seemed to benefit more from the experience, while I adopted the "I'm just doing this for my mom" attitude. Parental support can be a mixed blessing."*
>
> **Recent Grad,**
> **University of Wisconsin - Oshkosh**

▶ KEEP TRACK OF YOUR FINANCIAL AID

Even if your parents are paying a big chunk of your tuition or giving you extra spending money, it's still your responsibility to keep track of all of your financial aid, look for scholarships, and stay out of credit card debt. So get on top of it all and stay there.

- Check in with the financial aid office often and know when you have to re-file any forms or submit any applications.

- Continue to look for new scholarships even after you start college and make yourself apply for as many as possible.

- Stick to your budget and if you get into money trouble, get help and get it fast.

You can do it—you just have to get organized and understand what's involved. Hopefully we've been able to shed some light on that in this book.

▶ TALK TO YOUR PARENTS

You may have noticed that this seems to be a common theme throughout this book. That's because we think that there's a lot to be gained from communicating with your parents frequently and openly. Make sure you're in agreement about who is paying for what, and about whether you will owe them for their expenses. If they send you money, know whether it's a gift or a loan.

But most importantly, go to your parents for help if you need it. Don't worry that they will think you're not responsible enough to handle your own finances. In fact, it's just the opposite—admitting that you need advice or help is very responsible. Your parents have been managing their own finances for years—they have bank accounts and credit cards, they earn their own money at their jobs, they've paid countless bills. Take advantage of the wealth of knowledge they have and ask their advice on anything from choosing a credit card to opening a bank account to grocery shopping. They will be more than willing to help.

▶ REMEMBER THAT YOU'RE NOT ALONE

Millions of college students each year fill out financial aid forms, get confused by scholarship applications, live on a budget, skip going out to save a few bucks to pay the phone bill, charge too much on their credit card, and do all of the things that you'll probably do—and be frustrated by—once in a while. The fact that all of those other smart and bright students make the mistakes that you make means that you're not stupid and you're not alone. It's all part of a learning process and the struggle to manage the continuously rising costs of a college education. You're awesome for even attempting to do it.

what "they" say

We asked several high school guidance counselors and college financial aid advisors for their advice to students embarking on the battle to get through college without going broke.

Here are some suggestions that they wanted to share with you:

WHAT IS IMPORTANT FOR A SOON-TO-BE COLLEGE STUDENT TO KNOW ABOUT PLANNING FINANCIALLY FOR COLLEGE?

"Students sometimes have unrealistic ideas about what they can afford to pay for a college education. I encourage students and their parents to have conversations about this early on—sophomore, junior year—and to discuss what types of family funds are available."

**Guidance Counselor,
Barnstable High School**

"Students need to request of their parents a serious and realistic conversation about financing college before the application process begins. Although many parents take on this responsibility themselves, I've discovered that some parents do not."

**Guidance Counselor,
Henderson High School**

"If your high school has a good career center specialist (or whoever first receives financial aid information in your building), become friends with that person. Our career center specialist gets to know the kids who come forward, and as she gets info on specific aids, she actually thinks of and sends for these kids based on their circumstances, qualifications, etc. Many students don't realize that such personal contacts do make a big difference."

**Guidance Counselor,
Annandale High School**

"Each year I counsel several traumatized seniors whose four years of hard work are rewarded by admission to elite, expensive colleges, and whose dreams are shattered and families thrown into turmoil when a dismal financial reality hits. This could (and should) be avoided—first, by a realistic discussion of college finances no later than the junior year (initiated by the student, if necessary), and second, by consideration given to a family's bottom-line financial situation when applying for schools."

**Guidance Counselor,
Henderson High School**

WHAT ADVICE DO YOU HAVE ABOUT BEING FINANCIALLY SMART WHEN APPLYING FOR COLLEGES?

"Students need a "financial safety" college—a college they know they will be accepted at, and can afford, should the financial aid they need not be forthcoming. Students can apply to any range of colleges based on cost, but they need to have that financial safety college as a backup. This avoids a crisis in the senior year when a student and the

family do not have enough finances to pay for the colleges to which they were accepted."

**Guidance Counselor,
Barnstable High School**

"There are many smaller, less publicized private colleges that offer excellent education. In competition with better-known schools, they may offer great scholarships or financial aid for students whose stats (GPA, SAT scores, etc.) are solid, or who bring unique characteristics that the school is looking for. Name recognition is NOT everything! And there ARE ways to go to a private college even if you are not wealthy."

**Guidance Office,
Annandale High School**

"The most common mistake that students make is to self-select themselves out of applying to high-cost, highly selective schools simply because of the cost. Most schools in this group offer financial aid solely on the basis of financial need, and meet that need fully. Because of the sizable scholarship endowment of these schools, in many cases, especially for high need students, the financial aid packages may make one of these schools more affordable than less expensive schools."

**Financial Aid Advisor,
Vassar College**

WHAT SHOULD COLLEGE STUDENTS, OR SOON-TO-BE COLLEGE STUDENTS, KNOW ABOUT FINANCIAL AID?

"Do some homework and know at least a little about financial aid. You can meet with your financial aid advisor to ask some questions and get an idea of how things work. The more knowledgeable you are the better!"

**Financial Aid Advisor,
SUNY - Cortland**

"Everyone should apply for financial aid no matter what their family income is. Fill out the required forms and then be told that your family makes too much money—if you don't apply, you will not be considered for any form of financial aid like merit awards, work-study, or loans from a particular college."

"Be cautious with college scholarship services—most of them charge high fees and one can find the same resources in high school guidance counselors' offices, online, or in the community library. Students can search for their own scholarships—it is time consuming but in the long run it might be worth it in terms of money for college."

**Guidance Office,
Monroe-Woodbury High School**

"Find out if you have an assigned financial aid counselor and meet them. Get to know them. They can be helpful to you throughout your college career."

"Meet with your financial aid advisor at least once each semester, if not more, to make sure your aid is in place

and that you have satisfied any outstanding requirements. You don't want to be shocked that you still owe a bill at the end of a semester, are put on a stop list, and won't be allowed to register for classes."

"Start searching for scholarships during your junior year in high school and continue the search right up through your junior year in college. That way you are prepared and will know what scholarships you are eligible for in advance."

"Do not pay anyone to file your FAFSA form for you. It's called the FREE application for Federal Student Aid. Any financial aid counselor will assist you with the form. You can also do it online!"

**Financial Aid Advisor,
SUNY - Cortland**

"Be sure to read college publications for the DUE DATE of application materials for financial aid. The money awarded, especially at private institutions, is limited and late filers can be denied simply because they failed to meet required deadlines."

**Financial Aid Advisor,
Lehigh University**

HOW CAN STUDENTS BEST MANAGE THEIR MONEY IN COLLEGE?

"Once on campus, start operating on a budget."

"Use debit cards instead of credit cards—that way you're spending money already in the bank and not running up a credit card balance which you'll be unable to pay monthly."

"Students should start some savings program monthly—even if it's putting away something as small as $10—it gets you in the habit of putting money away for rainy days!"

**Guidance Counselor,
Monroe-Woodbury High School**

"[After getting a credit card] students find themselves in trouble because they don't realize (at least some of them) that monthly payments will be required, and failure to make payments jeopardizes their credit rating (for up to 7 years) as well as incurs an incredible amount of interest. Even making minimum payments on small debts can take years to repay. Parents and students need to talk about using credit cards and "true emergencies" for their use."

**Financial Aid Advisor,
Lehigh University**

helpful resources

Here are some other helpful resources you should consider during your quest to figure out how to pay for college and graduate without too much unnecessary debt.

☞ WEBSITES

▶There's no need to pay anyone to find scholarships appropriate for you.

www.fastweb.com is the most popular and the largest database of scholarships. Start here before you try anything else.

▶The following sites all have free scholarship searches:

www.collegenet.com
www.absolutelyscholarships.com
www.nationalmerit.org
www.scholarships.com

▶If you're feeling overwhelmed, confused, or just curious, go to any of these sites for general advice and information on financial aid:

www.finaid.org is a clear, helpful, and specific website. Give it a shot.

Other useful sites are:

www.collegeboard.com
www.ed.gov/studentaid

►Before you apply for a scholarship, check with the Better Business Bureau on the background of the company or organization offering the scholarships and make sure it's legitimate:

www.betterbusinessbureau.com or **www.bbb.com**

►If you're interested in taking out a government loan to finance your education but would like more information first, you can find it here:

www.dlservicer.ed.gov

►Fill out the Free Application for Federal Student Aid online and get help with it at:

www.fafsa.ed.gov

►Fill out the PROFILE online at:

profileonline.collegeboard.com

►Here are a few of the websites that we've found helpful to buy (and sell) textbooks and many other items for school:

www.bigwords.com
www.bn.com
www.ecampus.com
www.half.ebay.com
www.varsitybooks.com

☞ PHONE NUMBERS

Federal Student Aid Info Center:

1-800-4-FEDAID (333243)

Call the Direct Loan Servicing Center for information on your particular loan:

1-800-848-0979

☞ PRINTED RESOURCES & BOOKS

►Check your guidance office or financial aid office for these two booklets, put out by the U.S. Department of Education each year. They hold a wealth of information about federal aid programs and guidelines:

The Student Guide

Funding Your Education

►Here are a few helpful books you might want to consider:

How to Go to College Almost for Free, by Ben Kaplan. Harper Collins, 2001.

Get Free Cash for College, by Kelly Y. Tanabe, Gen S. Tanabe. Supercollege, LLC, 2001.

The College Board Scholarship Handbook 2002, by College Board (editor). College Board, 2001.

☞ PEOPLE AND OFFICES

▶Your **guidance or financial aid counselor** should have loads of information on applying for financial aid, finding scholarships and loans, getting a job, or anything else you're having problems with.

▶Your campus **career services office** can help you find jobs and internships, critique your resume and cover letter, and give you tips on successful interviews.

▶Check with your local **military recruitment office** for more information on the various options the military offers to help finance your education.

the final word

Well, now you're all set! You have a full scholarship for college, a great job, and a ton of money to spend on whatever you want. Right?

Well, probably not, but that's OK. The reason we wrote this book wasn't to tell you how to get all of that—hey, if we knew that, we'd be off vacationing in Hawaii—but to offer you some advice, taken from our own experiences and the experiences of dozens of other students, on how to find a way to survive college without going completely broke.

Paying for college is difficult, and it requires a tremendous amount of effort and willpower. We've been there, we've made mistakes, and we're still learning. Know that you're not alone in your efforts, that you're pretty awesome for taking responsibility and tackling the tough task of getting through college on a budget, and that you're learning things along the way that will make your life easier once you graduate.

Good luck!

To learn more about **Students Helping Students™** guides, read samples and student-written articles, share your own experiences with other students, suggest a topic or ask questions, visit us at **www.StudentsHelpingStudents.com**!

We're always looking for fresh minds and new ideas!